THE GOD QUESTIONS

EXPLORING LIFE'S GREAT QUESTIONS ABOUT GOD

HAL SEED
DAN GRIDER

OUTREACH®

The God Questions Revised Edition

Copyright © 2018 by Hal Seed and Dan Grider

Published by Outreach, Inc., Colorado Springs, CO 80919

www.Outreach.com

ISBN: 9781942027935
Cover Design: Tim Downs
Interior Design: Alexia Garaventa
Editing: Jennifer Dion, Toni Ridgaway, Tia Smith

CONTENTS

HOW TO GET THE MOST OUT OF THESE QUESTIONS

The God Questions is designed to give you answers to your deepest spiritual questions. I've discovered two things from conducting surveys over the last twenty-five years: (1) *everyone* has questions about God, and (2) while there are dozens of minor questions about Him, there are six major questions that pretty much everyone asks. Once you understand the answers to these six, you will not only have the answers for your personal faith, you'll find yourself able to help your friends with their questions as well.

The Design of This Book

The God Questions is designed with six weeks' worth of readings for individual study, for study with a small group, or as part of a church-wide campaign. The book is divided into six sections of questions, with six short chapters per question. To get the most out of the book, I encourage you to cover one section per week. Reading a chapter each day will leave you with a seventh day to participate in a small-group discussion each week.

The Small Group Discussion Guides at the back of the book are designed for a group Bible study in conjunction with *The God Questions'* daily chapter readings. There is one guide per major question. Encourage each group member to read the chapters on that major question so they can come prepared to enter into a lively conversation.

Church leader resources are available at Outreach.com.

QUESTION #1
IS GOD REAL?

CHAPTER 1

WHERE DID THE WORLD COME FROM?

(PART 1)

*The heavens declare the glory
of God; the skies proclaim the
work of his hands.*

—Psalm 19:1

Throughout human history, people have questioned the existence of God. We can't see, hear, feel, touch, or taste Him, so how can we really know if He exists? It's such an important question that scholars have given it deep thought over the ages. Many have concluded that there are sound reasons to believe in Him. I'll give you five of them; together these form a compelling argument that God is real. They'll even point you toward the kind of God He is.

Reason #1: The Universe

The universe itself is a powerful pointer to the existence of God. It's big and beautiful, and all of its parts work together well. Its very existence raises the following question: "How did the universe get here?" Think about it: If nothing existed, would you have to explain it? Of course not! But the moment something exists, a question can be raised of its origin. The attempt to answer this question has led many scientists to conclude that God must exist.

The most obvious answer to "How did the universe get here?" is, "It came from something else." Animals come from their parents, plants come from seeds, houses come from a builder, and cars come from factories. In fact, *everything* in the universe comes from something else. Everything you see, touch, taste, feel, and smell is *contingent* on something that came before it.

Not only that, everything that exists is *dependent* on something else. Humans depend on food for nourishment. Plants depend on the sun for photosynthesis. The sun depends on gravity to keep from breaking apart. So everything in the universe came from something else, and everything is dependent on something else in order to exist.

Push way back into the history of the universe and ask, "Where did all of this stuff come from?" The answer most people come to is "God." Everything in the universe was created by something else and depends on something else. The cause of all of this must be something that is uncreated and independent— or, in positive terms, something that is *eternal* and *self-sufficient*. The only being that could fit such a description is God.

Another way to think about this is to view the universe as one big object. Using your mind as a camera lens, zoom out so far that you capture everything in the universe in the circle below. Everything inside the circle is contingent and dependent.

THE UNIVERSE

In Question #5, I'll present evidence that suggests the universe has not always existed. Assuming that to be true for the time being, because the universe is not eternal, it must have come from something that is non-contingent and non-dependent. Those two terms come very close to a working definition of God.

The Bible says, *"The heavens declare the glory of God; the skies proclaim the work of his hands. . . . They have no speech, they use no words; no sound is heard from them. Yet their voice goes out into all the earth, their words to the ends of the world"* (Psalm 19:1, 3–4). God is communicating to us through what we see in the universe! He's saying, "I am here. I exist. You can tell, because I made this place."

"The first question which should rightly be asked is: Why is there something rather than nothing?" G. W. Leibniz

---

Everything that's been made must have a maker. The French skeptic Voltaire once said, "I shall always be convinced that a watch proves a watch-maker." In the same way, the existence of the universe proves the existence of God.

CHAPTER 2

WHERE DID THE WORLD COME FROM?

(PART 2)

In the beginning you laid the foundations of the earth, and the heavens are the work of your hands.

—Psalm 102:25

Reason #2: The Creator

Lori and I (Hal) keep a special box in a cabinet in our garage. It contains scores of pictures our daughter Amy drew as a little girl. It's not hard to guess how old Amy was at the painting of each picture. Some look like they were painted by a four-year-old, others by an eight-year-old, still others by a sixteen-year-old. You can tell a lot about a creator by studying what she (or he) has created. This illustrates the second evidence of the existence of God: Every design reflects its designer.

Chart the path of the stars, measure the decay rate of an atom, examine the laws of physics: Everything you study is well-ordered, precise, and complex. Stare up into the night sky, walk a beach at sunset, put a snowflake under a microscope; everywhere you look, our world is saturated with beauty. This beauty and complexity in the universe point not only to a Creator but also to the nature of the Creator: ingenious, beautiful, and detailed.

Plato decided it was reasonable to believe in God based on "the order of the motion of the stars, and of all things under the dominion of the mind which ordered the universe."[1] Isaac Newton said, "When I look at the solar system, I see the earth at the right distance from the sun to receive the proper amounts of heat and light. This did not happen by chance."[2]

The Pepsi Can[3]

Imagine that sitting on the desk in front of me is a Pepsi can. How did it get here?

Here's a theory: Millennia ago, a huge explosion sent a small meteor spinning through space. As it cooled, a caramel-colored, effervescent liquid formed on its surface. As time passed, aluminum crept out of the water and shaped itself into just these dimensions. Over time, this thing formed itself a one-time retractable lid, from which a crease appeared, a bit off-center, and out of it grew a pull tab. Centuries later, red, white, and blue paint fell from the sky and clung to its exterior, forming the letters P-e-p-s-i on its surface.

"The mathematical precision of the universe reveals the mathematical mind of God."
Albert Einstein

This Pepsi can fits perfectly in the palm of the normal-sized human hand. Its volume is just right for satisfying one person's desire for something sweet and liquid. It has just enough caffeine to pep you up, but not so much that you realize you're actually in an artificially induced state of stimulation. Its contents are always the same. Its quality never varies.

How many scientific explanations about the nature of matter and the origins of the universe would I have to give to convince you that the Pepsi can happened by chance? What are the odds that something this complex, useful, comfortable, and attractive came about as a result of a random collision of molecules? The can is too carefully designed to be the result of chance or coincidence. Some very smart people thought deeply about the design and manufacture of this can.

The Banana

Now, hold a banana in your hand. Notice the banana fits perfectly in your palm. In fact, it fits better than the Pepsi can. It's been thoughtfully made with a nonslip surface. It comes with a time-sensitive indicator on the outside to let you know the condition of the contents before you even open it: Green means "keep going," yellow means "slow down and eat it," and black means "too late, make banana bread."

The banana's top contains a pull tab for convenient opening. Ease back firmly on the tab, and it peels neatly according to its premade perforations. If it's at just the right stage for eating, it even gives off a little "click" sound as it's opened. The wrapper peels into four pieces and hangs gracefully over your hand. Unlike the Pepsi can, this wrapper is environmentally sensitive, made completely of biodegradable substances that in time enrich the soil it nestles in.

The fruit is the perfect size and shape for the human mouth, with a point on the top for easy entry. It is full of body-building calories and is easy for the stomach to digest. And the Maker of the banana has even curved it toward the face to make the whole eating experience easier and more pleasant.

No wonder the Bible says about God, *"Your workmanship is marvelous"* (Psalm 139:14, NLT). From looking at the design of the banana, I conclude that there is a God; that He is brilliant, creative, and thoughtful; and that He loves to delight people through all five of our senses!

CHAPTER 3

WHY IS THERE MORALITY?

Indeed, when Gentiles, who do not have the law, do by nature things required by the law, they are a law for themselves, even though they do not have the law. They show that the requirements of the law are written on their hearts, their consciences also bearing witness, and their thoughts sometimes accusing them and at other times even defending them.

—Romans 2:14-15

Reason #3: Our Sense of Morality

In my youngster days, my mom and I (Hal) had a tradition. We would go to the store, and if I was a good boy, she would buy me a treat. One of the saddest days of my life was the day that all changed. I remember it vividly. We were standing in the checkout line, and I put my candy bar on the conveyor belt.

"No," she said, "I'm not buying you a treat today."

"Why not? I've been a good boy."

"I'm just not, that's all."

Because she had no good reason *not* to get me the candy bar,

I saw no good reason not to get it for myself. I pretended to take it back to the candy aisle, but instead, I buried it in my pants pocket.

Can you guess why I remember that day so vividly? Yep, I got caught. When we got home, I snuck off by myself and pulled out that candy bar. Moms have a sixth sense about certain things. My mom's was so sharp, it was like she had a *seventh sense*. She confronted me with a wad of chocolate in my cheek.

"What are you eating?" she asked.

"A candy bar."

"And where did you get it?"

"At the grocery store."

"And how did you pay for it?"

"I didn't."

What followed was a lesson I have never forgotten. We drove back to the store and located the manager. I was made to confess my crime, apologize sincerely, and make financial restitution. I was embarrassed, humiliated, and ashamed all at the same time.

Did I learn my lesson? Yes and no. Yes, I learned that crime doesn't pay. And no, I didn't learn to be absolutely honest from that day forward. The truth is, when I took that candy bar, I *already* knew I was taking something that didn't belong to me. I knew what I was doing was wrong, but I did it anyway.

I've done it since then too. I haven't stolen any more candy bars, but I have taken things that didn't belong to me. Pens from my employer, copies for personal use. And I've done worse. I've said things that weren't true in order to make myself look better. I've done things to other people that I knew would hurt them. I identify with the Apostle Paul: *"I don't understand myself at all, for I really want to do what is right, but I can't. I do what I don't want to—what I hate. I know perfectly well that what I am doing is wrong. . . . But I can't help myself"* (Romans 7:15–17, TLB).

From time to time, I'll ask people in my church, "How many of you have never said anything that you knew wasn't true or taken something that didn't belong to you?" No one raises their hand. We're all guilty. We all have a moral standard that we believe in but can't seem to live up to. Paul said, *"It seems to be a fact of life that when I want to do what is right, I inevitably do what is wrong"* (Romans 7:21, TLB).

"If no set of moral ideas were truer or better than any other, there would be no sense in preferring civilized morality to savage morality, or Christian morality to Nazi morality. The moment you say one lot of morals is better than another, you are in fact measuring them by an ultimate standard." C. S. Lewis

---

How many times have you started to do something, and an alarm goes off in your head whispering, "Don't do that!" but you do it anyway? How many times have you opened your mouth, and your conscience murmurs, "Don't say it!" but you say it anyway? You know what the right thing is, even if you don't always do it. Where did that sense of "right" come from? This is the third reason to believe in God: *We all have a moral standard that is higher than ourselves.*

Ethical codes vary from person to person and culture to culture, but every human being has an innate moral standard. Where did this standard come from? Because it's impossible to invent something that is greater than we are, *there must be a moral Creator who put this standard within us.*

CHAPTER 4

WHO IS JESUS?

The Son is the radiance of God's glory and the exact representation of his being.

—Hebrews 1:3

Reason #4: Jesus

One of the greatest evidences of the existence of God is the life of Jesus Christ. Jesus claimed to be God.[4] Some people struggle with this claim because there are only two possibilities for it: Either it's true, or it's not true. If it's true, He is Lord and God. If it's not true, there are only two possibilities. One is, His claim was false, and He knew it. The other is, His claim was false, and He didn't know it. If it was false and He knew it, that would make Him a liar. If it was false and He didn't know it, that would make Him a lunatic. (Any person who really believes he is God must be clinically insane.) This is what's known as "The Trilemma."[5] It presents us with three choices—Jesus was the Lord, a liar, or a lunatic.

C. S. Lewis, who was once an avowed agnostic, saw the reasoning behind this and eventually became a Christian. Afterward, he wrote,

> *A man who was merely a man and said the sort of things that Jesus said would not be a great moral teacher. He would either be a lunatic—*

on a level with a man who says he is a poached egg—or else he would be the Devil of hell. You must make your choice. Either this man was, and is, the Son of God: or else a madman or something worse.[6]

Moses, Muhammad, and Joseph Smith claimed to be prophets. Buddha, Confucius, and Lao Tzu were silent on the idea of God. Only Jesus claimed to be God in the flesh.

Most people who dismiss the resurrection of Christ do not take the time to look closely at the facts. Those who honestly study this unique event conclude, like C. S. Lewis, that no one but God Himself could pull off such a miracle. So consider the following biblical account of the facts, corroborated by the historical knowledge of ancient Roman practices and other first-century records.

On Good Friday, Pontius Pilate had Jesus flogged thirty-nine times with a cat-o'-nine-tails.[7] The severity of this beating left His flesh in ribbons and His organs exposed.[8] A crown of thorns was placed on His head,[9] and a 110-pound crossbeam, called a "patibulum," was placed on His shoulders.[10] Jesus had spent His first thirty years as a carpenter, but this whipping left Him too weakened to carry the lumber all the way up the hill.

A bystander named Simon of Cyrene was involuntarily recruited to carry the crossbeam up the hill.[11] Upon reaching Golgotha, guards nailed Jesus's wrists to the patibulum and His feet to the upright stake and raised Him vertically, where He hung from 9 a.m. to 3 p.m. He was pronounced dead by a professional Roman executioner, who verified His death by piercing His heart with a spear.[12] This centurion was so impressed with the way Jesus endured His execution that he remarked, *"Truly this was the Son of God!"* (Matthew 27:54, NASB).

In keeping with Jewish custom, Jesus's body was washed on a stone table in a burial chamber. Joseph of Arimathea volunteered his personal tomb for this purpose. The tomb had been recently hewn out of solid rock.[13]

He was washed with warm water and packed in one hundred pounds of spices.[14] His body was wrapped in no fewer than three separate burial garments,[15] and a 1.5- to 2-ton stone was placed in front of the tomb's entrance.[16] Pilate ordered a guard unit[17] to make the area *"as secure as you know how"* (Matthew 27:65).[18] The guards sealed the stone to the tomb[19] with clay packs and stamped it with Pilate's official signet ring. Because of what they had witnessed, the disciples were despondent and fearful.[20] When reports of Jesus's resurrection came in, they refused to believe He was alive.[21]

If Jesus didn't rise from the dead, His disciples would have known it. Of the original twelve disciples, Judas Iscariot hanged himself, believing that his betrayal caused Jesus's death.[22] John died in exile in modern-day Turkey. The other ten were all put to death for their faith. Sometimes good men will die for a good cause, but how likely is it that many would die for a lie?

"Yes, if the life and death of Socrates are those of a philosopher, the life and death of Jesus Christ are those of a God." Jean-Jacques Rousseau

---

Jesus's tomb had been officially sealed. The penalty for breaking a Roman seal was crucifixion upside down.[23] Who would have the courage or motivation to do this? The huge stone covering the tomb had to be rolled *uphill* to open the tomb entrance. Who would have the strength and numbers to do this? The Roman guard unit was trained to hold their ground against an entire battalion. Who could have overcome them?[24] When Mary, Peter, and the others viewed the grave clothes, they saw that they were undisturbed (except the face cloth, which was rolled up in a place by itself).[25] The linen wrappings were lying on the table in the form of a body, slightly caved in and empty. How did that happen?

Five people examined the tomb and found it empty on that first Easter Sunday morning.[26] Over the next forty days, Jesus appeared to more than 515 eyewitnesses.[27] These eyewitnesses were from various stations in life and various states of disbelief. But what they witnessed caused them to share the story of Jesus's resurrection with as many people as they could. What can explain this?

CHAPTER 5

WHAT ABOUT MY EXPERIENCE?

Now I know that there is no God in all the world except in Israel.

—2 Kings 5:15

Reason #5: Personal Experience

On January 20, 1971, I (Hal) visited a Christian coffeehouse with some friends. I was not a Christian at the time. During the ride there, my coach, Dick Roth, used a phrase that struck me as odd. "I talked to God this morning," he said.

The idea of having a personal conversation with God seemed so absurd to me that I laughed out loud. Two hours later, on the drive home, Dick asked if I wanted to begin a personal relationship with the Lord. I said, "I do." What happened to me? I had an experience with God at that coffeehouse. I saw evidence of His real presence in the lives of the people there. And I experienced His personal presence for myself.

This whole idea of a personal relationship with God was so new to me that the next morning I wondered if the whole thing had been real. I asked out loud, "God, are You really there?" Immediately I sensed Him saying, "Yes, I'm here." At the same moment, I felt light chills run down my spine. A hundred times since then I have whispered that same, "God, are You really there?" Each time He responds, "Yes, I am," accompanied by those same chills. Really. It's been happening for me now for forty-five years.

How do I explain that? Some might say, "Well, you just *wanted* to believe." But I didn't. I was content with my life. I was minding my own business, enjoying being a teenager. What happened was this: During the meeting that night, I experienced enough evidence to convince me that there was a real God who wanted a real relationship with me. I invited Him to be the Lord and leader of my life. The minute I did, I experienced Him up close and personal.

The Bible says that everyone can have an experience with God if they seek Him sincerely. *"Ask and it will be given to you; seek and you will find; knock and the door will be opened to you"* (Matthew 7:7). It also says that all humans were made to experience God, that God has *"planted eternity in the human heart"* (Ecclesiastes 3:11, NLT).

King Nebuchadnezzar of Babylon was one of the most powerful men of the first millennium BC. Ascending the throne in 605 BC, he conquered a ridiculous amount of territory. To please his favorite wife, he built the Hanging Gardens of Babylon, one of the Seven Wonders of the Ancient World. Nebuchadnezzar was a polytheist, believing in a whole pantheon of gods. His story makes its way into the Bible because, at a critical juncture in his life, he had an experience with God that left him saying, *"Then I praised the Most High; I honored and glorified him who lives forever. His dominion is an eternal dominion; his kingdom endures from generation to generation"* (Daniel 4:34).

"I believe in Christianity as I believe that the sun has risen, not only because I see it, but because by it I see everything else." C. S. Lewis

---

Around 825 BC, the commander of the Syrian Army was a general named Naaman. In the midst of a stellar military career, Naaman contracted leprosy. Like Nebuchadnezzar, Naaman's belief system was that of his surrounding culture. He was an animist, believing that many gods inhabited various geographic features (rivers, mountains, the sky, etc.) and performed the functions necessary for life on earth (moving the sun across the sky, making rain, etc.). Attempting to find a cure for his leprosy, Naaman ventured outside of his theological comfort zone and sought the God of Israel. God healed Naaman. Based on this experience Naaman said, *"Now I know that there is no God in all the world except in Israel"* (2 Kings 5:15).

What happened to both of these men? They each had a personal experience with God. Experience is strong evidence of the existence of God. It is *subjective* evidence, not *objective*, because you can't replicate it in a laboratory. But the fact that so many people in so many ages have experienced God in a meaningful way is hard to argue with and harder still to explain—unless God is real.

Years ago, a landscape architect named Greg started attending my church. "I'm an atheist," he announced somewhat proudly. Greg and I started having lunch together weekly, working through the evidences of God you've been reading about in these first few chapters. One afternoon Greg said to me, "Actually, all of my life I have felt like God has had His hand on my shoulder." Since then I have met hundreds of people who could say the same thing. I believe that, in their heart of hearts, most people have experienced the subtle presence of God in their lives during quiet moments of pain or contemplation.

During lunch that day, Greg reached out to God just as God had been reaching out to Greg. The two of them have been doing life together ever since.

Anthropologists tell us that every culture on earth has held a belief in some type of God. People tend to view *experience* as a weak argument for believing in God—until they reach out and have the experience for themselves. Then it becomes the most compelling reason of all.

CHAPTER 6
IS THERE ANY PROOF
I CAN TOUCH?

*Faith shows the reality of
what we hope for; it is the evidence
of things we cannot see.*

—Hebrews 11:1 (NLT)

Even in matters of faith, we want proof. In December 2002, Rev. Cliffe Knechtle and Dr. Michael Newdow held a nationally broadcasted debate. Knechtle is a staff member at InterVarsity Christian Fellowship. Newdow is an atheist attorney and physician. Dr. Newdow had recently gained national notoriety for suing the U.S. government to have the words "under God" removed from the Pledge of Allegiance. The subject of the debate was "Is God Real?"

Several times during the debate, Knechtle referred to evidence similar to what we've been exploring over these first several chapters. None of it convinced Newdow. Newdow consistently cited the one reason that kept him from believing: He could not see, hear, touch, taste, or smell God.

Newdow was holding out for *scientific proof* for the existence of God. "If I can't see Him, I can't believe in Him," he reasoned.

Is his request reasonable? Yes and no. Yes, it is reasonable to expect evidence for the things we believe. In a court of law, no one is convicted based on hearsay; substantiated proof is required. But no, wanting scientific proof is not reasonable in a case like this, because this is not a case where science is of most help. Scientific proof is based on replicating a process or event multiple times in a controlled environment. Science is based on a belief that *natural laws* are always at work, so each time we repeat an experiment, we should get the same results. The problem is, God isn't merely *natural*; He's *super*natural.

Suppose a careful scientist were to set up a controlled experiment to test for God. Suppose he says, "I will believe in God if, right now, He causes this cup I'm holding to disappear." Suppose the cup disappears. Then what? If the scientist genuinely believes that supernatural phenomena are impossible, he will look for an explanation for the cup's disappearance that doesn't include God. His explanations might include, "Someone was playing a trick on me," "The cup never actually was there," or "The cup still is there, and my mind is playing a trick on me."

"The solution of the riddle of life in space and time lies outside space and time."
Ludwig Wittgenstein

On the other hand, suppose our scientist concludes that the cup really has disappeared. If he's like most of us, five minutes after its disappearance he's going to say, "Could that have really happened?" Based on the scientific principle of uniformity of results, he'll rerun the experiment to verify it. Suppose God makes the second cup disappear too. The scientist then publishes his results, and others replicate the experiment in their own labs. If the cup doesn't disappear for these scientists, scientist #1 is declared a nutcase, and the whole thing is forgotten. If the cup disappears each and every time, the scientific community declares that there is a natural phenomenon to account for it and begins developing a new theory of physics to explain it.

Physical investigation, by its very nature, can't verify the existence of nonmaterial things. *Reason, history,* and *experience* are the appropriate truth tests to apply to a search for a spiritual being. Why these tests? (1) Because God Himself is reasonable. (2) Because He claims to have appeared in history. And (3) because He can be experienced by people.

I Get to Use My Brain

Christianity joyfully declares that the God who created human intelligence never asks us to leave it at the door. Jesus encouraged everyone to love God, not only with their hearts and souls but also with their minds.[28] Romans 1:20 proclaims that God has deliberately placed evidence of Himself throughout the universe so that we can discern His invisible attributes and divine nature. Psalm 19:1 celebrates God's constant communication to His creation. No one has to express *blind faith* or even merely *sincere faith.* Human beings were created with a capacity to perceive the spiritual realm.[29] One day we will be able to grasp it even more fully. First Corinthians 13:12 says, *"Now we see only a reflection as in a mirror; then we shall see face to face."*

What's at Stake?

Some people have a strong desire to believe in God. They want assurance that they're not alone in this world. Other people have an equally strong desire *not* to believe in God. The thought of an all-powerful Creator is threatening to them. Yet, if there really is a Creator, then everything you can see, hear, touch, taste, feel, or imagine is His property. In fact, *you* are His property.

When I (Hal) was a little guy, my parents built a swimming pool in our backyard. Whenever the pool deck got wet, it got slippery, so my parents made a rule to keep us safe: *No running on the pool deck.* In all our years of having guests over, no one ever objected to my parents' rule. Why? It was their pool. They built it, they maintained it, and they *owned* it. An owner has the right to make reasonable rules and expect guests to follow them.

The decision to believe or not believe in God should not be based on a vested interest. It ought to be based on evidence, experience, and reason. How objective are you about weighing the evidence for and against God? Romans 1:20 explains that *"ever since the world was created, people have seen the earth and sky. Through everything God made, they can clearly see his invisible qualities—his eternal power and divine nature. So they have no excuse for not knowing God"* (NLT).

The Nature of Faith

Everyone exercises faith. All day, every day. When your alarm goes off in the morning, you get up believing that you still have a job to go to. You brush your teeth, believing this will keep your teeth healthy and alleviate bad breath. At the office, you sit down in a chair, believing it will support your weight like it always has. A client asks a question and you answer it, believing that you understood her question. Everything you experience is based on faith. You have no absolute assurance of anything, *only belief based on evidence.*

So, when it comes to believing in God, where does the majority of the evidence point? To summarize this week's readings:

- A creation requires a Creator.
- An intelligent design requires an Intelligent Designer.
- A sense of moral standards points to a Moral Standards Giver.
- The evidence for Christ's deity suggests there must be a Deity.

- My personal experience tells me there is a God who loves me.

Is God real? The Bible says, *"Only fools say in their hearts, 'There is no God.' . . . The* LORD *looks down from heaven on the entire human race; he looks to see if anyone is truly wise, if anyone seeks God"* (Psalm 14:1–2, NLT). There really is a God, and He really is here with you now.

CHAPTER 7
IF GOD IS REAL, HOW CAN HE IMPACT MY LIFE?

"God said, 'I will live with them and walk with them, and I will be their God, and they will be my people'."
—2 Corinthians 6:16-17

From my (Dan's) home near the California coast, I can regularly see a cluster of hot-air balloons. Before a balloon is launched, the ground is covered with a limp, colorful canvas that begins to ripple and take form when the burner is fired up. The hot air slowly fills the cloth. Before long, the air lifts the balloon off the ground, where it hovers ready for flight until its earthbound tether is released. Soon, all can enjoy the beautiful sight of exploding colors as many balloons hang in the sky.

Much like those hot-air balloons, individuals who are pursuing God remain earthbound until their tethers are no longer grounded. Just as the rope holding the balloon must be released or cut, so too must one cut his/her ties with earth, so that the "God experience" is not simply another item on one's to-do list.

If we spend our lives pursuing the answers to spiritual questions, there will come a time in which we realize that the answers alone will not leave a lasting satisfaction. Metaphorically speaking, finding answers to our questions will not make us airborne. It takes something far more powerful than a piece of missing information; we must find something that will produce lasting life change. A critical step to living the life of a Christ-follower is to receive the power of God through the Holy Spirit.

The Bible tells us that God has shown Himself to us in three ways: God the Father, God the Son and God the Holy Spirit, collectively referred to as the "Godhead." One early Christian leader described the three entities of the Godhead to be like water. Water that is placed in a freezer becomes a solid; it is hard and firm. Ice best illustrates God the Father, who is solid, immovable, holds the universe together and provides order. Water poured into a glass will take the shape of the glass, just as God the Son took the shape of a human body and became one of us. Finally, God the Holy Spirit is as water placed in a heating teapot. Before long, the steam shoots across the room and gently lands upon everything in its realm. The steam cannot be traced or located. God has planned for the Holy Spirit to be the agent of change for Christ-followers, and our behavior changes when the Holy Spirit dwells within us.

When I was 25 years old, I became a pastor of a small, rural church. During that first year, I was befriended by a member named Jim, who was a church leader and the town doctor. One day, Jim put his arm around me and said, "I really like you, but you are going to get disillusioned and be disappointed." Puzzled, I asked Jim what he meant, and he said, "You really believe that people will change. People seldom ever change. They keep on making the same mistakes. Liars keep on lying, greedy people stay greedy and adulterers keep on committing adultery. I just hate to see you have your bubble burst."

When I think about what Jim said, I must agree with him. Apart from the transforming power of Christ, we are unable to change. Perhaps you have previously attempted to make behavioral changes but felt helpless and unable to make those changes last. Without the Holy Spirit within us, we are unable to truly modify our behavior. Now, the question is not "Will I change my behavior?" but rather "Will I allow the Holy Spirit of God to change my behavior?"

Over the course of this study, we have investigated the claims of Christ, authority of Scripture and the nature of God. Now we must embrace God in all His forms. If you have been drawn to trust God, I hope that you respond to the growing revelation of who He is. When we embrace Him, He gives our lives a new motivation and purpose. As the Father, Son and Holy Spirit, He has an impact on us and changes our behavior.

The amazing truth that comes from the Bible is that God the Father has provided a way for each of us to change and receive a new life. The Bible tells us, *"We are God's workmanship created in Christ Jesus to do good works."* [11] Again, God does not simply extend this plan as a casual take-it-or-leave-it affair; He expects us to fully embrace this mission.

The apostle and Biblical writer Paul says, *"I plead with you to give your bodies to God. Let them be a living and holy sacrifice—the kind he will accept. When you think of what he has done for you, is this too much to ask… let God transform you into a new person by changing the way you think. Then you will know what God wants you to do and you will know how good and pleasing and perfect his will really is."* [12]

This verse reminds us that God desires to change and transform us into His plan and purpose for us. Paul is begging us to use this life to glorify God. Paul knows the fleeting nature of our lives on earth. In addition, he realizes that the greatest tragedy in life is not death, but a life that is lived without reflecting the likeness of the Father. Our behavior can only change when we allow God the Holy Spirit to do the transforming work in us.

QUESTION #2
IS THE
BIBLE TRUE?

CHAPTER 8

WHERE DID THE BIBLE COME FROM?

*The law of the LORD
is perfect.*

—Psalm 19:7

The Bible is not a mysterious book. It *contains* mysteries, but once you know how it's laid out, the book itself is not mysterious.

The Bible Is a Collection

Technically, the Bible is not a book; it is a book of books. It's a compilation of sixty-six different books written over a period of 1,500 years, in three different languages, on three different continents, with consistency of message, and without contradictions. The books of the Bible are ordered as follows:

Old Testament		
History	Poetry	Prophecy
Genesis	Job	Isaiah
Exodus	Psalms	Jeremiah
Leviticus	Proverbs	Lamentations
Numbers	Ecclesiastes	Ezekiel
Deuteronomy	Song of Songs	Daniel
Joshua		Hosea
Judges		Joel

Old Testament (Continued)		
History	Poetry	Prophecy
Ruth		Amos
1 Samuel		Obadiah
2 Samuel		Jonah
1 Kings		Micah
2 Kings		Nahum
1 Chronicles		Habakkuk
2 Chronicles		Zephaniah
Ezra		Haggai
Nehemiah		Zechariah
Esther		Malachi

New Testament			
History	Letters		Prophecy
	From Paul	From Others	
Matthew	Romans	Hebrews	Revelation
Mark	1 Corinthians	James	
Luke	2 Corinthians	1 Peter	
John	Galatians	2 Peter	
Acts	Ephesians	1 John	
	Philippians	2 John	
	Colossians	3 John	
	1 Thessalonians	Jude	
	2 Thessalonians		
	1 Timothy		
	2 Timothy		
	Titus		
	Philemon		

Open a Bible to its Table of Contents, and you'll see that it's divided into two major sections: the Old Testament with thirty-nine books, and the New Testament with twenty-seven books. The Bible is further divided into types of literature. The Old Testament has three sections, containing *history* (Genesis through Esther), *poetry* (Job through Song of Songs), and *prophecy* (Isaiah through Malachi).

"There exists no document from the ancient world witnessed by so excellent a set of textual and historical testimonies and offering so superb an array of historical data on which an intelligent decision may be made." Clark Pinnock

---

The Jews (including Jesus) often referred to their Bible as *"the Law of Moses, the Prophets and the Psalms"* (Luke 24:44), reflecting these three sections, or often just as *"the Law and the Prophets"* (Matthew 7:12). The New Testament also contains three sections: *history* (Matthew through Acts), *letters* (Romans through Jude), and *prophecy* (the book of Revelation).

Who Wrote the Old Testament?

The earliest-written book in the Bible is maybe the book of Job. Some scholars believe Job lived around 1900 BC, in which case the Bible's authorship actually spans a full two thousand years. Job's closest rival for first authorship is Moses, who recorded the history of the people of Israel around 1400 BC. The first five books of the Bible are called "The Books of Moses." Moses could not have written the final few verses of Deuteronomy, since they describe his death and succession. Joshua may have written the ending as a tribute to his leader.

Moses most likely copied the first eleven chapters of Genesis from a previous source. At the very least, the entire book of Genesis would have existed in the oral teachings of the Hebrews long before Moses was born.

During the late 1800s, skeptics of the Bible claimed that Moses could not have written these books, because *writing* wasn't invented until after his death. This caused quite an embarrassment in 1901 when Jacques de Morgan and Jean-Vincent Scheil excavated the ancient city of Susa and discovered the Code of Hammurabi etched in a stone tablet. Hammurabi lived in 1795 BC.

Deuteronomy 31:26 tells us that, when the Tabernacle was first constructed, the writings of Moses were placed inside the Ark of the Covenant in a sacred room called the Holy of Holies. As more Scriptures were produced, they were placed there as well. Later, when the Temple was built in Jerusalem, the Ark and the Scriptures were moved there.

Joshua deposited the book that bears his name.[30] Samuel wrote *"on a scroll and deposited it before the LORD"* (1 Samuel 10:25) as well, including the books of Judges, Ruth, and most of the first book of Samuel. Samuel, the last of Israel's judges and the first of the line of prophets, established a school of prophets[31] who carried on his work of recording the history of God's people. These writers included Nathan and Gad,[32] Ahijah and Iddo,[33] Jehu,[34] Isaiah,[35] and others.[36]

Scholars believe that Jeremiah was the prophet who completed the books of Kings,[37] along with the book of Lamentations and the book of Jeremiah itself. Ezra the scribe compiled the books of Chronicles for the benefit of the Israelites, who returned to the land following their exile to Babylon. He also authored Ezra and enlisted Nehemiah's help in composing the book of Nehemiah. Tradition says that Mordecai, Esther's relative, wrote the book of Esther.

Half of the Psalms are attributed to King David. King Solomon wrote the books of Ecclesiastes, Song of Solomon, and most of Proverbs. According to the Talmud (the author-itative Jewish commentary on the Old Testament) and the first-century historian Josephus, the succession of the writing prophets ended in Nehemiah's day, with the final prophet being Malachi.[38]

The Old Testament Scriptures produced after the Temple was built in Jerusalem were kept together in the Ark. During the time of the exile in 586 BC, the Temple was destroyed and the original copies were lost forever. The scrolls used in producing today's Bible translations are copies that were in circulation at the time the originals were lost.

Thus, the Old Testament was completed about 400 BC. This begins what is known as "the four hundred years of si-lence."[39] Much of what happened in Israel during this "Intert-estamental Period" (the time between the two testaments) was written down, but there were no authoritative prophets, so the writings of this period do not bear the marks of canonicity.[40] In other words, these writings do not have the authority and inspi-ration of Scripture.

Who Wrote the New Testament?

Almost half of the New Testament's twenty-seven books are let-ters written by the Apostle Paul as a means to instruct Christians and young churches on how to live the Christian life.[41] One of Paul's close followers, the Gentile doctor Luke, wrote Luke and Acts. The Apostle John wrote five New Testament books (1, 2, and 3 John, the Gospel of John, and Revelation). Two were written by Peter, and one by his close follower, Mark.

Of the remaining four books, one was written by the Apos-tle Matthew, and two others by Jesus's half brothers, James and Jude. The book of Hebrews is believed to be a sermon preached somewhere in a local church. Its authorship has been widely de-bated; some believe it was a sermon of Paul's, others say it came from Apollos. One intriguing theory is that it was written by Priscilla, a female leader of the early church, who did not identify herself to keep the book from suffering gender bias. All of the New Testament's books were written between AD 46 and 90.

So What?

Ephesians 2:20 says that the Christian church is *"built on the foundation of the apostles and prophets."* The Bible claims authority based on many factors we'll explore in the next few chapters. The first of these is the authorship factor. Each of the sixty-six books of the Bible was written either by a prophet (someone who heard from God, whose credentials were recognized and affirmed by their contemporaries and by history), an apostle (one who had been an eyewitness of the risen Christ), or someone with direct linkage to one or the other.

CHAPTER 9

HOW IS THE BIBLE DIFFERENT FROM OTHER BOOKS?

Your laws endure to this day, for all things serve you.

—Psalm 119:91

The Bible is unlike any other book in the world. It was the first book printed on a printing press. In fact, Johannes Gutenberg's major motivation for creating the printing press was to produce copies of the Bible. It is also the most expensive book in the world. Greatsite Marketing's website offers one "leaf" (meaning "page") of an original Gutenberg Bible for the asking price of $95,000 to $195,000. It estimates the worth of a complete 1455 edition at $100 million.[42] The Bible was also the first book translated into another language. Greek-speaking Jews translated it from Hebrew to Greek in the third century BC in a manuscript called "the Septuagint." The longest telegram in history is the Revised Version of the New Testament, sent from New York to Chicago.[43] The largest first-edition printing of any book in history was a Bible; 1.2 million copies were made, and the entire run sold out before printing![44]

The Bible Is Unique
The 1960s were turbulent times for the United States. The young Baby Boomer generation was questioning not only the

Vietnam War but everything authoritative, traditional, or created by the "establishment." During this time, a young former atheist named Josh McDowell stepped onto college campuses. In his personal quest for truth, McDowell did research into the Bible. He finally concluded that the Bible is the most unique piece of literature in all of history.

"It isn't the parts of the Bible that I can't understand that bother me, it is the parts that I do understand." Mark Twain

---

McDowell's lectures on college campuses drew tens of thousands of students and faculty. The outline of his message was simple: The Bible is unique in its continuity, circulation, translation, survival, and teaching. His main message to audiences was, "If you are an intelligent person and you are searching for the truth, you will read this one book that has drawn more attention than any other."[45]

Unique in Its Continuity

As I mentioned, the Bible was written across continents and in multiple languages over a span of well over a millennium. The diversity of its forty contributing authors includes poets, peasants, philosophers, and kings writing in a variety of moods ranging from the thrill of victory to the agony of defeat. Yet it remains consistent in its message and has no contradictions. No other book can boast this.

But the most impressive thing about the Bible's continuity is its unity. The Bible addresses hundreds of controversial issues yet agrees substantially on every issue, from cover to cover. In spite of the differing circumstances under which the books were written, one theme progressively unfolds from one book to the next: God's building of community with mankind. Can you imagine picking forty authors today, all from the same time period, all speaking the same language, all from the same nation, all writing on the same topic, and having them all agree on even *one* controversial issue—say, embryonic cell research? Or premarital sex? Or the war on terrorism? Could you even ask them to write a coherent essay together on one theme? Such a book seems impossible.

Unique in Its Circulation

The Bible is the best-selling book of all time. It has been the best seller each and every year since 1455 when the printing press was invented. From 1810 to 1990, International Bible Society sold or gave away 300 million Bibles in 450 languages. Since 1981, 150 million copies of the Bible have been purchased. In the weeks following the attacks of September 11, 2001, 800,000 copies were donated and distributed throughout the New York City area.[46] In 2003 alone, the United Bible Societies sold or gave away 21.4 million Bibles, 14.4 million New Testaments, and 400 million selected Scriptures—more than *430 million* in total.[47] What other book comes close to this kind of circulation?

Unique in Its Translation

As of 2014, portions of the Bible have been translated into 2,883 languages, representing more than 95 percent of the population of the earth. In 1999, Wycliffe Bible Translators announced an initiative to have the Bible translated into every remaining language community by 2025. As of 2012, Bible translators were working on portions of Scripture for 2,075 languages.[48] What other book comes close?

Unique in Its Survival

Because papyrus, vellum, and paper are all perishable, the Bible has been recopied countless times over the last 3,500 years, yet its accuracy is uncanny. Professor and apologist Bernard Ramm explained the process the Old Testament went through:

> *Jews preserved it as no other manuscript has ever been preserved. With their massora (parva, magna and finalis) [methods of counting] they kept tabs on every letter, syllable, word and paragraph. They had special classes of men within their culture whose sole duty was to preserve and transmit these documents with practically perfect fidelity—scribes, lawyers, massoretes. Who ever counted the letters and syllables and words of Plato or Aristotle? Cicero or Seneca?*[49]

John Warwick Montgomery described the reliability of the New Testament text this way:

> *To be skeptical of the resultant text of the New Testament books is to allow all of classical antiquity to slip into obscurity, for no documents of the ancient period are as well attested bibliographically as the New Testament.*[50]

Add to this that no other book has suffered the kinds of attacks the Bible has. From ancient Rome to modern communism to Islamic states, the Bible has been banned, burned, outlawed, and restricted. Yet it remains the most widely circulated and read book in the world. In fact, the Bible is so resilient that people who forecast its demise usually end up as anecdotes of history. For instance, in 1778, the French skeptic Voltaire predicted that within one hundred years of his time, Christianity would be nonexistent. Fifty years later, the Geneva Bible Society used his house and printing press to produce stacks of Bibles![51] In AD 303, Emperor Diocletian ordered that all copies of the Christian Bible be destroyed in his realm. Nineteen years later, in AD 322, Emperor Constantine ordered fifty copies of the Bible be made—at government expense! What other book can make such claims?

Unique in Its Teaching

The Bible is the only book that boldly exposes itself to potential disproof by making specific predictions about the future. There are more than 2,500 prophecies in the Bible; 2,000 have already come true.[52] The other 500 remain for the future.

The Bible is the only book of antiquity that teaches history with such accuracy. It presents a clear picture of tribal and family origins.

> *In Egypt and Babylonia, in Assyria and Phoenicia, in Greece and Rome, we look in vain for anything comparable. There is nothing like it in the tradition of the Germanic peoples. Neither India nor China can produce anything similar, since their earliest historical memories are literary deposits of distorted dynastic tradition, with no trace of the herdsman or peasant behind the demigod or king with whom their records begin. Neither in the oldest Indic historical writings (the Puranas) nor in the earliest Greek historians is there a hint of the fact that both Indo-Aryans and Hellenes were once nomads who immigrated into their later abodes from the north.*[53]

The Bible is the only book that treats miracles in a matter-of-fact way. Other books of antiquity describe miraculous events with flowery and superfluous language. In contrast, when Moses parted the Red Sea, the Bible simply says, *"Moses stretched out his hand over the sea, and all that night the* LORD *drove the sea back with a strong east wind"* (Exodus 14:21). When Jesus turned water into wine, the text says, *"Jesus said to the servants, 'Fill the jars with water'; so they filled them to the brim. Then he told them, 'Now draw some out and take it to the master of the banquet'"* (John 2:7–8). Instead of describing the miracle, it describes the miracle's effect on the master of the banquet! The Bible is the only ancient book that teaches with such humility.

It also treats its heroes with disarming honesty. It tells of Abraham's dishonesty, Moses's reluctance, David's adultery, Peter's denial of Christ, Paul's persecution of the Church, and Jesus's desire to avoid the agony of crucifixion. Where other books paint the best side of their subjects, the Bible deliberately shows real people with frailties and struggles.

None of these unique elements proves that the Bible is true, but they offer tremendous motivation to intellectually honest people. The Bible's promise is that *"you will know the truth, and the truth will set you free"* (John 8:32). Its pages call out enticingly, "Come and read. There is no other book like this one!"

CHAPTER 10

WHAT ABOUT ERRORS IN THE BIBLE?

When [the king] takes the throne of his kingdom, he is to write for himself on a scroll a copy of this law, taken from that of the Levitical priests. It is to be with him, and he is to read it all the days of his life.

—Deuteronomy 17:18–19

People ask me, "With all of the times the Bible has been copied from one language to another, how can we really be sure what it says?" Whenever that question comes up, my first thought is always, "If you only knew . . ." Our perception of history is a funny thing. Sometimes we assume that the details we don't know are unknowable. Then one day we read an article, hear a lecture, or read a book, and all of a sudden, a light goes on!

The Bible is the most accurately transmitted book of all time. Its transmission from one generation to the next has been done so carefully and is so well documented, once people know the whole story, they often remark that only God could have done such a brilliant job.

The Number of Translations

A common misperception is that if the Bible has been translated into so many languages, it must have been translated from one language to another, then another. Like the child's game of "telephone," where a roomful of kids sit in a circle and one whispers in the ear of the next, while the message gets progressively garbled as it moves from ear to ear. If the original message was "The duck is brown," the final message becomes distorted into something like "Danny loves Susie."

Transmitting a message from one person to another, or from one source to another, invites errors to creep in. And with the subtle shift of meaning that comes when a message is transmitted from one language to another, you can see how distorted a message could become over a 3,400-year period. This is why Bible scholars consistently translate from the original languages of Hebrew (99 percent of the Old Testament), Aramaic (mostly Ezra 4:8–6:18; 7:12–26; and Daniel 2:4–7:28), and Greek (the New Testament). They take great pains to ensure that the original text is the most reliable version possible.

"There is a Book worth all other books in the world." Patrick Henry

---

How the Old Testament Was Transmitted

Moses, the author of the first five books of the Bible, finished his writing by saying in Deuteronomy 32:46–47, *"Take to heart all the words I have solemnly declared to you this day, so that you may command your children to obey carefully all the words of this law. They are not just idle words for you—they are your life."* Over the centuries, the Jewish people were careful not only to teach the Bible to their children, but they treated the text itself like it was their life.

The Talmidim

The *Talmidim* (Hebrew for "students") shepherded the transmission of the Torah (Old Testament) from AD 100–500. They had great reverence for the Scriptures in their care. As a result, their process was meticulous. Synagogue scrolls had to be written on specially prepared skins of clean animals and fastened with strings taken from clean animals. Each skin had to contain a certain number of columns. Each column had to have between forty-eight and sixty lines and be thirty letters wide. The spacing between consonants, sections, and books was precise, measured by hairs or threads. The ink had to be black and prepared with a specific recipe. The transcriber could not deviate from the original in any manner. No words could be written from memory. The person making the copy had to wash his whole body before beginning and could work only when in full Jewish dress. The scribe had to reverently wipe his pen each time he wrote the word "God" (*Elohim*) and wash his whole body before writing God's covenant name, *Yahweh*.

The Masoretes

The *Masoretes*, who oversaw the Torah from AD 500–900, adopted an even more elaborate means of ensuring transcriptional accuracy. They numbered the verses, words, and letters of each book and calculated the midpoint of each. When a scroll was complete, independent sources counted the number of words and syllables forward, backward, and from the middle of the text in each direction to verify that the exact number had been preserved. Proofreading and revision had to be done within thirty days of a completed manuscript. Up to two mistakes on a page could be corrected. Three mistakes on a page condemned the whole manuscript.

These scribes treated the text so reverently that older manuscripts were destroyed to keep them from being misread.

Prior to 1947, the oldest extant Hebrew manuscript was from the ninth century. The discovery of the Dead Sea Scrolls enabled scholars to check the accuracy of current manuscripts against ones from 100 BC. When they compared the 100 BC scrolls to the ninth century manuscripts (a one-thousand-year gap), they found that an astounding 95 percent of the texts are identical, with only minor variations and a few discrepancies. In addition to Hebrew manuscripts, we have numerous ancient copies of the Septuagint, the Greek translation of the Old Testament dating from the second century BC.

How the New Testament Was Transmitted

The story of the New Testament's preservation is equally impressive. Historians use three criteria to evaluate the reliability of a historical text.

1. The number of manuscripts available. The greater the number of manuscripts, the better the ability to compare and reconstruct the original.

2. The time interval between the date of the original writing and the date the particular manuscript was made. The shorter the time interval, the closer to the actual events and eyewitnesses, and the fewer times the manuscript would have been recopied.

3. The quality of those manuscripts. The more legible the words on the page, the more accurate the reading and comparison with other texts.

Historians have a high degree of confidence that Julius Caesar conquered Gaul because we possess ten ancient manuscripts of Caesar's writings on the Gallic Wars. We have a high degree of confidence that Socrates lived, taught, and was executed by drinking hemlock because we possess seven ancient manuscripts of Plato's *Tetralogies*, in which he documents the death of his beloved mentor and teacher.

Consider the following chart:[54]

Author	When Written	Earliest Copy	Time Span	Number of Copies
Caesar	100–44 BC	AD 900	1,000 years	10
Plato	427–347 BC	AD 900	1,200 years	7
Tacitus	AD 100	AD 1100	1,000 years	20
Thucydides	460–400 BC	AD 900	1,300 years	8
Herodotus	480–425 BC	AD 900	1,300 years	8
Aristotle	384–322 BC	AD 1100	1,400 years	49

Of all ancient Greek and Latin literature, Homer's *The Iliad* ranks next to the New Testament in possessing the greatest amount of manuscript testimony.[55] Here is how it compares to the New Testament:

Homer (*Iliad*)	900 BC	400 BC	500 years	643
New Testament	AD 40–100	AD 125	25 years	24,000

In terms of quality of manuscripts, Ken Boa wrote, "While the quality of the Old Testament manuscripts is excellent, that of the New Testament is very good—considerably better than the manuscript quality of other ancient documents."[56]

So What?

By all standards of scholarly accuracy and reliability, the Bible stands head and shoulders above all other literature in history. In the entire New Testament, only four hundred words are in question (0.5 percent). The variants for these words are so slight that no doctrine of Christianity is affected by the potential alterations in meaning.

CHAPTER 11

IS THE BIBLE TRUE?

There is a God in heaven who
reveals mysteries.
—Daniel 2:28

Some of my friends have an insatiable need for evidence. Theories, hypotheses, and even logic don't move these "show me" types. They need factual proof. God understands that. After all, He wired them that way. So, for my friends (and the others like them), there exists tangible evidence for the veracity of the Bible. The authenticity of the Bible gets a huge vote of confidence from three surprising sources: *science, archaeology,* and *prophecy.*

Evidence from Science

The Bible is not a scientific textbook, but it does describe how the universe works. Consider the following:[57]

What the Bible Says	What People Thought	What We Now Know
Earth is a sphere	Earth is a flat disk	Earth is a sphere
Number of stars = more than a billion	Number of stars = 1,100	Number of stars = more than a billion
Every star is different	All stars are the same	Every star is different
Light is in motion	Light is fixed in place	Light is in motion
Air has weight	Air is weightless	Air has weight
Winds blow in cyclones	Winds blow straight	Winds blow in cyclones
Blood is a source of life and healing	Sick people must be bled	Blood is a source of life and healing

For centuries, scientific theory was at odds with the Genesis 1 description of the physical and biological development of Earth. Today, scientists are in substantial agreement with the initial conditions of Genesis 1, as well as with subsequent events and the order in which they occurred.[58] The likelihood that Moses, writing 3,400 years ago, could have guessed all these details is infinitesimal.

In addition to the phenomena just mentioned, the Bible describes:

- The conservation of mass and energy[59]
- The hydraulic cycle of evaporation, condensation, and precipitation[60]
- Gravity[61]
- The Pleiades and Orion as gravitationally bound star groups[62]
- The effect of emotions on physical health[63]
- The spread of contagious disease by close contact[64]
- The importance of sanitation to health[65]

What grade would you give a book that could do this and was completed two thousand years ago?

Having investigated the evidence, astronomer and skeptic Robert Jastrow concluded,

> For the scientist who has lived by his faith in the power of reason, the story ends like a bad dream . . . he is about to conquer the highest peak [of scientific truth]; as he pulls himself over the final rock, he is greeted by a band of theologians who have been sitting there for centuries.[66]

Evidence from Archaeology

During the late nineteenth century, Western scholars began excavating locations throughout the ancient Near East. By

1950 more than 25,000 sites had been explored,[67] revealing and confirming much about biblical history. Discoveries from these sites provide a second piece of tangible evidence to support the trustworthiness of the Bible by corroborating biblical accounts with archeological findings.

Excavations at the cities of Mari, Nuzi, and Alalakh verify that Abraham's customs were consistent with his eighteenth-century BC culture. Excavations at Hazor, Gezer, Megiddo, and Jerusalem confirm the account of Joshua's conquest of Canaan, David and Solomon's building of the United Kingdom, the demise of power during the Divided Kingdom, and the Babylonian Exile.

Many key finds have so reshaped our understanding of history that they have been given their own unique and specific names. For instance, the "Moabite Stone" gives information about the reign of King Omri.[68] "The Black Obelisk" depicts Assyrian king Shalmaneser III's triumph over King Jehu.[69] The "Taylor Prism" describes Sennacherib's siege of Jerusalem while Hezekiah was king.[70] And the "Lachish Letters" shed light on Nebuchadnezzar's invasion of Judah.[71]

"Through the wealth of data uncovered by historical and archaeological research, we are able to measure the Bible's historical accuracy. In every case where its claim can be thus tested, the Bible proves to be accurate and reliable." Jack Cottrell

---

One of the more intriguing archeological finds is John Garstang's excavation of the city of Jericho in 1930. Joshua 6:20 indicates the walls of Jericho collapsed in a way that enabled the Israelites to charge straight into the city. For years, skeptics cited this as an example of biblical inaccuracy because city walls do not fall outward; they fall *inward* when they collapse, leaving the town in rubble. Guess what Garstang found? The walls fell outward! This finding was so unexpected that he and two other colleagues signed a statement verifying it.[72]

According to the book of John, one of Jesus's great miracles was the healing of the cripple at the Pool of Bethesda.[73] Outside of the New Testament, no evidence had ever been found for such a pool. Thus skeptics pronounced John's writing inaccurate, "the obvious work of an imposter." Then, in 1888, traces of the pool were discovered near the church of Saint Anne.[74] I've actually visited the pool.

Luke gave specific names of rulers, officials, and events, providing ample fodder for criticism. He described an enrollment of taxpayers.[75] He identified Quirinius as governor of Syria.[76] He listed Lystra and Derbe as cities in the province of Lycaonia,[77] and Lysanias as tetrarch of Abilene.[78] Each of these was called into question by skeptics of the Bible. Yet over time, each of Luke's statements has been verified by archaeological findings. Archeologist Dr. Joseph Free wrote, "Archaeology has confirmed countless passages that have been rejected by critics as unhistorical or contradictory to known facts."[79]

Evidence from Prophecy

From Moses to Malachi, the role of the prophet was critical to the spiritual and moral health of Israel. God wanted His people to be convinced when someone was speaking for Him, and the Bible lays out a simple test to determine a prophet's authenticity: 100 percent accuracy. *"If what a prophet proclaims in the name of the LORD does not take place or come true, that is a message the LORD has not spoken. . . . But a prophet who presumes to speak in my name anything I have not commanded . . . is to be put to death"* (Deuteronomy 18:22, 20).

Can you imagine the boldness of predicting the name and foreign policy of a U.S. president 150 years from now? In 700 BC, Isaiah did something like this. He predicted that Jerusalem would be surrounded and its people carried into captivity.[80] His prophecy was fulfilled one hundred years later. He went one step further in predicting the Israelites' return to their homeland *and* the ruler who would set them free: *"I will raise up Cyrus in my righteousness. . . . He will rebuild my city and set my exiles free"* (Isaiah 45:13). History verifies that Cyrus, the founder of the Persian Empire, reigned from 559–530 BC and that he issued a decree in March 538 BC that allowed the Jews to return to their homeland. Skeptics have found it so unbelievable that a man could predict the name of his country's liberator a century before it needed liberating that they have mounted an attack on the book of Isaiah itself, proposing that this prophecy must have been written or inserted by someone living in Cyrus's day, or later.

Ezekiel made an equally startling prediction about the city-state of Tyre (in modern-day Lebanon). He prophesied that:

- Many nations would come against Tyre (Ezekiel 26:2).
- Nebuchadnezzar would destroy the city (Ezekiel 26:4).
- The city would be scraped bare (Ezekiel 26:4).
- Fishing nets would be spread over the site (Ezekiel 26:5).
- The stones of the city would be thrown into the sea (Ezekiel 26:12).
- The city would never be rebuilt (Ezekiel 26:14).

Here's what happened: Tyre was a city in two parts. Half the city lay on the coast, the other half on an island one-half mile from shore. The historian Josephus records that Nebuchadnezzar besieged the coastal city for thirteen years and finally captured it.[81] Many of its citizens escaped to the island, which remained unconquered. Two hundred forty years later, Alexander the Great attacked the island city.[82]

To get from the mainland to the island, Alexander constructed a causeway using the rubble from the old coastal city as his building material. He literally *"scrape[d] away her rubble and ma[d]e her a bare rock"* (Ezekiel 26:4). He also used ships to attack from the sea. The ships were manned by people from the nations he had already conquered, including 80 from Sidon, Aradus, and Byblos; 10 from Rhodes; 10 from Lycia; and 120 from Cyprus.[83] The city of Tyre has never been rebuilt. There is a small town on the island today. Fishermen from the town spread and cast their nets from the barren rocks.[84]

The Old Testament contains hundreds of prophesies related to the coming Messiah; 332 of these were fulfilled in Christ's first coming.[85] (I've listed sixty-one of them in the endnotes.[86]) Using the mathematical science of probability, author Peter Stoner, an academic in the areas of science and mathematics, calculated the odds that any one person could fulfill just eight prophesies predicted of the Messiah. After doing his calculations, he said, "We find that the chance that any man might have lived down to the present time and fulfilled eight prophecies is 1 in 10^{17}" (1 in 100,000,000,000,000,000).[87]

To illustrate that probability in practical terms, Stoner used the following illustration:

> *Supposing we take 10^{17} silver dollars and lay them on the face of Texas. They will cover all of the state two feet deep. Now mark one of these silver dollars and stir the whole mass thoroughly, all over the state. Blindfold a man and tell him that he can travel as far as he wishes, but he must pick up one silver dollar and say that this is the right one. What chance would he have of getting the right one? 1 x 10^{17}.*[88]

Calculating the probability that someone could fulfill forty-eight prophecies gave Stoner the number 1×10^{157}. The number of atoms in the universe has been calculated at 10^{80}.

CHAPTER 12

WHAT DOES THE BIBLE SAY ABOUT ITSELF?

And the words of the LORD are flawless, like silver purified in a crucible, like gold refined seven times.

—Psalm 12:6

The Bible makes bold claims for itself. It claims to be *"active"* (Hebrews 4:12), authoritative (see Deuteronomy 32:46–47), enduring (see Psalm 119:91), *"flawless"* (Psalm 12:6), *"good"* (Psalm 119:39), instructive (see Psalm 119:24), *"perfect"* (Psalm 19:7), powerful (see Jeremiah 23:29), revelatory (see Exodus 24:4), *"trustworthy"* (2 Samuel 7:28), and more. Are these claims true?

In chapter 10, we looked at evidence from outside sources; today, we'll look *inside* the source and examine some of what the Bible says about itself. Someone might call this circular reasoning: "You can't judge a book by what it says about itself!" In a court of law, defendants take the witness stand and testify for themselves all the time.

Two Claims

Let's examine just two claims the Bible makes:

1. It claims to be a road map for life (see 2 Timothy 3:16).

2. It claims to speak to us about our inner thoughts and motives (see Hebrews 4:12).

The Bible as a Road Map

The Bible says, *"All Scripture is God-breathed and is useful for teaching, rebuking, correcting and training in righteousness"* (2 Timothy 3:16). The Bible teaches by saying to its students, "Here is the road." It rebukes by saying, "Here is how you've gotten off the road!" It corrects and gives encouragement to get back on the road. And it trains in righteousness by pointing out how to get back on the road. Does the Bible fulfill these four functions?

"One of the many divine qualities of the Bible is that it does not yield its secrets to the irreverent and the censorious." James I. Packer

---

I (Hal) became a Christian when I was thirteen years old. Since that time, as I have read the Bible, it has defined right and wrong and good and bad for me. It has defined the road for my life, and it has also helped me see when I have gotten off the road. In fact, while friends and spiritual leaders have given me much input over the years, words from the Bible have most often convicted me when I've gotten off that road.

Since founding New Song Church in 1992, I've spent much of my time helping people who have lost their way or gotten off their road and want to know how to get back on it. Every week I open the Bible to prepare a sermon that will help people with practical answers for living a good life, and every week I find the answers I need in the Bible—answers that help people, practically and realistically. I've prepared more than a thousand sermons and never once lacked guidance.

Not only does the Bible define the road and how to get on it, its forte is helping people stay on the road. I have never come across a topic that the Bible does not address, either directly or in principle. Scripture contains principles and examples that pertain to everything you'll ever face. Financial difficulties? Parenting? In-laws? Out-laws? Sex? Abortion? Developing confidence? Handling loss? Growing old? Improving your attitude? Improving your IQ? Physical exercise? It's all there. Granted, I can only speak from my own experience, but survey one hundred serious Bible readers, and I think you'll find them agreeing with me. The Bible has proven itself to be a road map for everyone who turns to it for direction.

It Speaks to Me About Who I Am

Hebrews 4:12 says, *"For the word of God is alive and active. Sharper than any double-edged sword, it penetrates even to dividing soul and spirit, joints and marrow; it judges the thoughts and attitudes of the heart."*

My normal habit is to read a portion of the Bible every morning. When I do, it often stimulates a dialogue within me. Say I'm reading a portion of Scripture about the importance of being honest. As I read, I may be thinking, *"I'm a fairly honest person. There may have been a time when I was less honest. I'm sure glad this passage isn't speaking to me."* Then a second thought comes: *"Actually, you're not that honest. You want people to think better of you than you really are, so you tend to send signals or say things that lead people to think more highly of you than they should. This is something you should work on."*

What happened? My thoughts were "judged" by the words I was reading. This doesn't happen to me when I'm reading a novel or watching television, but it happens regularly when I read the Bible. As I compare my experience with friends, they affirm the same thing: The Bible speaks to us about who we really are.

Do these two claims constitute proof that the Bible is true? No. We would have to examine the claims of hundreds of Scriptures, one at a time, for that. But if the Bible is true, this examination is a worthwhile endeavor—a lifelong endeavor. And it's a logical pursuit for anyone who wants divine guidance for his or her life.

Summary

In the modern age, the primary test for truth was *logic*: "Things that are reasonable or provable are true."

In the postmodern age, the primary test for truth is *experience*: "Things that work for me are true." The most convincing postmodern proof of the Bible's veracity is locked inside the heart of those with direct experience reading, interacting with, and applying the Bible. Ultimately, no one can come to a conclusion about the Bible until he or she reads it.

CHAPTER 13

WAS THE BIBLE WRITTEN BY GOD OR MEN?

Above all, you must understand that no prophecy of Scripture came about by the prophet's own interpretation of things. For prophecy never had its origin in the human will, but prophets, though human, spoke from God as they were carried along by the Holy Spirit.
—2 Peter 1:20–21

The Bible is God's Word, but in what sense? Throughout the Bible, there are passages where the author said, "*The word of the* LORD *came to me*" (Jeremiah 1:11), or God said, "*Write down these words*" (Exodus 34:27). But there are other times when authors like Luke said, "*I . . . decided to write*" (Luke 1:3). So which is it? Were the human writers passive dictation machines, or did they write what they wanted to write? Two descriptions from biblical writers themselves help shed light on this question.

Inspiration and the Will of Man

The Apostle Paul wrote, "*All Scripture is inspired by God*" (2 Timothy 3:16, NASB). In the original Greek, the word "inspired" is *theopneustos*. Some versions translate it "God-breathed" or, more precisely, "God-exhaled." According to this verse, that which was written by biblical authors started in the mind of God.

Peter wrote in 2 Peter 1:20–21, "*No prophecy of Scripture came about by the prophet's own interpretation of things. For prophecy never had its origin in the human will.*" Peter was affirming that each writer was moved by God to write what God wanted written.

If God directed the writing process, why aren't all the writing styles alike? Isaiah wrote with confidence, Jeremiah with sorrow. John used very simple Greek; Luke used technical language. This raises three more questions:

1. Some parts of the Bible aren't original to the biblical writers. Joshua quoted the book of Jasher in Joshua 10:13; Jude quoted the book of Enoch in Jude 14. Paul quoted a hymn in Philippians 2:6–11, and he even quoted a pagan polytheist, Epimenides, in Acts 17:28. *Were these quotes "God-breathed" when composed by their original writers?*

2. Some portions of the Bible are written in prose. Others are written in poetry (Psalms), parables (Ezekiel 24:2), riddles (Proverbs 1:6), satire (Matthew 19:24), allegory (Galatians 4), or hyperbole (Matthew 5:29). *Why so much variety?*

3. Throughout the Bible there are descriptions that are scientifically inaccurate, like "sunrise" in Joshua 1:15 or "from one end of the earth to the other" in Deuteronomy 28:64. *How could God use language that He knew was wrong?*

Human Agency

God intentionally allowed human agency to play a role in the style and tone of the Bible. God superintended the content of what He wanted written through the unique personality of each anointed author. Biblical authors were not merely stenographers. In the process of inspiration, God guided the heredity, background, and time-in-history of each writer. So when writers recorded events, composed poems, and wrote allegories, the words used were their personal, conscious compositions guided by the mind of God.

Truth

Why are nonbiblical sources quoted in the Bible? Joshua and other biblical authors utilized historical sources *under the inspiration of the Holy Spirit* to record the truth of Israel's history. Jude used a source familiar to his audience (the book of Enoch) *under the inspiration of the Holy Spirit* to make the point that the Lord will return and judge the world. Likewise, Paul used the works of others *under the inspiration of the Holy Spirit* to convey the messages God had for His children.

God's Creativity

Why are there so many types of literature in the Bible? God inspired a variety of literature forms in order to speak to a variety of people. Plus, different forms of literature serve different purposes. Stories, which make up 40 percent of the Bible, paint pictures in our minds, imparting lessons that attach to those pictures. Instructional literature (like the letters of the New Testament) speaks truth straight to the mind on issues like theology and behavior. Prophetic literature requires concentration to understand, forcing the mind to think deeply, while poetic literature must be read slowly to appreciate the nuances. Apocalyptic literature unleashes the imagination and sometimes shocks us in a science-fiction-like manner. Each literary form touches or moves us in a different way. Some literary scholars believe the Bible is the archetype for every kind of literature known to man. The Bible is rich in its diversity of style, and like creation itself, this diversity reflects the creativity of God.

"I must confess to you that the majesty of the scriptures astounds me. . . . If it had been the invention of man, the invention would have been greater than the greatest heroes."
Jean-Jacques Rousseau

In the composition of Scripture, God breathed the truth He wanted to communicate into the minds of the people He had prepared. In this way, the words, forms, and concepts that were written down were fully His *and* fully theirs.

CHAPTER 14

IS THE BIBLE THE ONLY WAY GOD CAN MAKE HIMSELF KNOWN?

"The Lord...is patient with you, not wanting anyone to perish, but everyone to come to repentance."

—2 Peter 3:9

As a freshman in college, my (Dan's) dormitory floor was mostly populated by young men from Iran. Before that year, I had never met anyone of Persian descent, nor had I the opportunity to cultivate friendships with individuals whose faith tradition differed from my own. As I began to form relationships with these students, I would ask if they had ever been exposed to the message of Christ. Many admitted that they'd had very little exposure to the Christian faith; often they had come to the United States in search of a quality education and planned to return to Iran after graduation. I liked these guys and enjoyed their company, but I didn't know how to reconcile my Christian faith with their Islamic faith.

Moreover, I was bothered by the position that Jesus took in the New Testament book of John. In verse 14:6, Jesus said, *"I am the way, the truth and the life. No one can come to the Father except through me."* I realized that this verse seemed to exclude my new friends from eternal life. It's one thing to consider this verse in theory, but quite another to process it in light of real people who I had grown to know and love. But what bothered me the most was that these young men had not been given the same opportunity that I had to hear or understand the Gospel of Jesus, so how could they be held accountable for it?

In an effort to resolve this conflict, I decided to take a comparative religion class at the university I was attending. I hoped to find answers, but the class only caused me more confusion. Ironically, the crux of the dilemma came from the very words of Jesus Himself. He had made such a strong statement about salvation that it seemed there was no room for those who had never heard about him.

Making Himself Known

One day as I was reading Scripture, I discovered a passage in Romans that helped me find peace with my dilemma. Paul explains that each person has the ability to respond to God. In verse 1:19, Paul addresses the issue of people who have never heard the message of Christ. He says, *"What may be known about God is plain to them, because God has made it plain to them. For since the creation of the world God's invisible qualities, his eternal power and divine nature have been clearly seen, being understood from what has been made, so that people are without excuse."* [4]

It appears that God holds all of us accountable to respond to Him in a way that is aligned with our level of understanding of who God is. It says that all people are without excuse. Each of us must seek a relationship with God. The Bible indicates that God is most interested in our willingness to obey Him. For example, in 1 Samuel 15:22, Samuel says obedience is better than sacrifice. God is looking for people who will respond via relational obedience rather than in an impersonal, ritualistic way. The passage from Romans is prefaced with this: *"The wrath of God is being revealed from heaven against all the godlessness and*

wickedness of men who suppress the truth by their wickedness." [5]
Paul is warning us against blindly following a religion that suppresses the truth about the life-giving message of Christ. To do so would in fact be a rejection of all that Jesus did on our behalf. Here our problem is not one of lacking information; rather, it is one of willing rebellion—a lack of willingness to obey God's commands. Paul continues, saying,

> *"...they exchanged the truth of God for a lie, and worshiped and served created things rather than the Creator"...* [6] *We are reminded that, "since the creation of the world God's invisible qualities—his eternal power and divine nature—have been clearly seen, being understood from what has been made, so that men are without excuse. For although they knew God, they neither glorified him as God nor gave thanks to him, but their thinking became futile and their foolish hearts were darkened. Although they claimed to be wise, they became fools."* [7]

God calls every one of us, regardless of culture or religion, to respond to Him. The Bible says that we are responsible to respond to God at the level of our revelation, and all of us are without excuse. Obviously, a person who has received the full knowledge of Christ has become responsible to respond to the message of Jesus as the Bible reveals. However, a person who does not have an understanding of the message of Christ is only responsible to respond at the level of the revelation received, even if it is limited.

For instance, anyone who has lived in a remote area of the jungle, having never experienced anything beyond ancestor worship or superstitious responses, is still responsible in their heart to respond to God as He has revealed Himself in the created order. This allows them to still come to Christ, even though they've never heard of Christ. They must respond to God as dictated by their own revelation of the Almighty.

It appears then that God has not left Himself without a witness, for the book of Romans says that even the created order is the witness of Christ. When people know of Christ, and yet reject Him or the knowledge of Him, they have in effect rejected God's provision for them.

It is not wise to have the knowledge of Jesus Christ and His saving message and still adhere to the belief that all roads lead to heaven. Jesus never taught that this was a possibility. The Scripture says no one comes to the Father but by Him.

Imagine you took a trip to a national park with a group of friends. You began the day with great expectations and with the joy of seeing the beauty of the natural surroundings. But as the day continued, you became increasingly aware that you had lost your orientation. The group's joy came to a halt when everyone began to discuss the correct way back to the car. Everyone agreed the car was north, but each of you disagreed about which way was north.

Now let's say you had a compass with you. Even though everyone was adamantly declaring their particular direction as correct, you would not be considered hateful or intolerant if you shared with them your knowledge. The car is only in one location; the car cannot be in six locations. You possess a compass, which can direct you back in accuracy to true north, to exactly the place where the car is located.

Likewise, the truth of the message of Christ is uniquely different from the message of all other world religions. Even Jesus in His time was said to be One who was able to speak with authority, not like the religious teachers of the period. And so, just as knowing the true direction with the aid of a compass is not a bad or hateful thing, knowing the direction that God has given us is a beautiful revelation from God Himself.

Jesus clearly said that all roads do not lead to heaven. He said, *"Enter through the narrow gate. For wide is the gate and broad is the road that leads to destruction, and many enter through it. But small is the gate and narrow the road that leads to life, and only a few find it."*

Every person who has wrestled with the question of the fate of non-believers does so because they need to believe that God plays fair. But the Bible is clear that we each have God's fingerprint placed on our hearts, and we have an inherent moral obligation to respond to Him.

QUESTION #3
DO ALL ROADS LEAD TO HEAVEN?

CHAPTER 15

ISN'T "ONLY ONE WAY" TOO NARROW?

Jesus told him, "I am the way, the truth, and the life. No one can come to the Father except through me."

—John 14:6 (NLT)

One of the most passionate questions of belief has to do with *exclusivity.* Some people say Christianity is "too narrow." After all, what kind of a God would limit people to just one way of getting into heaven? Shouldn't He let all well-intentioned people join Him in the afterlife? Couldn't He be generous and broad-minded enough to let everyone in who tries? Aren't all religions pretty much the same when you get right down to it?

This idea has a long history. In AD 384, Christianity had become the favored religion of the Roman Empire, and Emperor Valentinian ordered the removal of the Altar of Victory from the Roman Senate. Symmachus, prefect of Rome, wanted to allow continued pagan worship in the Senate chambers. Notice his line of reasoning: "It is just that all worship should be considered as one. We look on the same stars, the sky is common, the same world surrounds us. What difference does it make by what pains each seeks the truth?"[89] In effect, Symmachus was arguing, "We're all human, and we're all seeking. Isn't that what counts? Since God is so kind and understanding, aren't *good intentions* what really matter to Him anyway?"

The Problem of Good Intentions

Good intentions have gotten me into trouble more times than I can count. When I (Hal) was in college, I had the best of intentions when I dove into the pool to lead off our school's four-hundred-yard freestyle relay at the National Championships. I was so amped up for the race that I forgot to drop my head as I hit the water. As a result, my goggles rolled off my eyes and settled around my mouth, producing drag and making it impossible to take a breath. Every time I turned my head to breathe, the goggles dumped water into my mouth, practically drowning me! My good intentions helped me swim hard, but they didn't help me swim fast. Not only did I pay for that mistake, the guys on my relay team suffered too. Good intentions coupled with poor methodology still made for a bad swim, a very upset coach, and several disappointed teammates. That day I learned that all my intentions can be good and sincere, but they can still be sincerely wrong.

"To maintain that all religions are paths leading to the same goal . . . is to maintain something that is not true. . . . The only common ground is that the function of religion is to provide release; there is no agreement at all as to what it is that man must be released from. The great religions are talking at cross purposes." R. C. Zaehner

---

All the major religions of the world ask their followers for sincerity. Each one also asks for exclusivity. Each one claims that their way is the only way. During these next several chapters, we'll explore the claims and paths of the world's largest religions. As you read, you'll see that there *can't* be two or more roads to heaven, because not only are the *roads* different but their *destinations* are different as well.

Why would God allow confusion like this? Why would a loving God visit one area of the world and describe one way to get to heaven, and then show up in another area and point them in a different direction? Answer: *He wouldn't.*

There Is a Deceiver

The Bible says in John 8:44 that there is another force at work in this world; Satan is a master of misdirection and misinformation. Jesus said, *"When he [the devil] lies, he speaks his native language, for he is a liar and the father of lies."* The last thing the Deceiver wants is for people to worship the One True, Living God. So if Satan can't keep us from worshiping God, he'll try to fool us into worshiping anything but God.

"Narrow" Is Not Always "Bad"

People sometimes accuse God of being cold and narrow because He has allowed only one way to get to heaven.

I felt a pain around my midsection one night. My wife called a nurse from our church, who sent her husband to drive me to the hospital. I was diagnosed with appendicitis. The doctor said the only way to relieve my pain was to have my appendix removed. "Is there anything I can do to avoid having an operation?" I asked.

The doctor answered, "Not if you want to live." It was a *very* narrow answer, but not once did I think he was cold or uncaring because he only gave me one solution to my problem.

Is God uncaring because He only gives us one solution? Consider this: Suppose that way back in time, a good and loving God created people in His own image. Suppose He gave those people free will so that they could make their own choices. Suppose He set them up in an idyllic environment with plenty of food and sunshine and interesting things to do. Suppose He imposed one restriction on them, warning them that if they violated the restriction, they would lose the gift of life He had given them.

Suppose His creation violated that restriction for no good reason, just because they felt like it. Suppose that, instead of taking their lives, God made provision for them and forgave them. Suppose that, despite God's provision, their descendants repeated that pattern over and over again.

Suppose that God bestowed special gifts on one particular nation so that they could know Him deeply and help others break their destructive pattern. Suppose this chosen nation rebelled too. Suppose that, time after time, God forgave this nation, delivered them from each threatening situation, and sent special messengers to communicate with them. Then suppose these people killed the messengers, turned their backs on their Creator, invented other religions, and worshiped stone idols and animals and mountains and rivers and streams.

Suppose, in an ultimate act of redemption, God Himself came to them in a human body as the Son of God, not to condemn them but to redeem them. Instead of welcoming Him, suppose the people rejected, tortured, and killed Him. Suppose that God accepted the death of His Son as payment for the sins of the very people who put Him to death. Suppose that God offered His Son's murderers complete forgiveness, transcendent peace, and eternal life as a free gift. Suppose God said, "I demand only one thing from you in return: that you honor My Son, who gave His life for you."[90]

If God did all this, would you still say, "God, You aren't being fair. You haven't done enough. I want another option"? The wonder is not *"Why is there only one way?"* It's *"Why is there any way at all?"*

CHAPTER 16

WHAT DO MUSLIMS BELIEVE?

You have heard that it was said, "Love your neighbor and hate your enemy." But I tell you, love your enemies and pray for those who persecute you.

—Matthew 5:43–44

Islam is the world's second-largest religion with 1.6 billion followers. The Islamic population is doubling every twenty-six years; the world's population is doubling every forty years.

History

Islam's founder, Muhammad, was born in the city of Mecca, near the coast of the Red Sea, around AD 570. His family was part of the Quraysh tribe, a minor branch of a Bedouin caste of merchant traders. At that time, the Arab people were polytheists, believing in many gods. According to some sources, they worshiped one god for each day of the year. Allah, the moon god, was one of those.

In 610, Muhammad had a visitation from one whom he believed was the angel Gabriel. The Koran states that the angel commanded him, "In the name of thy Lord the Creator, who created mankind from a clot of blood, recite!" (Sura 96:1). Muhammad recited, then described his revelations to his relatives and friends. He taught them that of all the gods they were worshiping, only the one they called "Allah" was the true God and demanded absolute submission to himself. In addition, Muhammad claimed that God had called him as Allah's last and greatest prophet.

"There is no god but Allah, and Muhammad is his prophet." First of the Five Pillars of Islam

---

View of God: Monotheism

Muhammad taught that there is only one God (Sura 2:133). He believed that Christianity's teaching of a Triune God (one God consisting in three Persons: Father, Son, and Holy Spirit) was a form of polytheism (Sura 5:73). Many Muslims today believe that Christianity's Trinity consists of God the Father, the Mother Mary, and their Son Jesus.[91]

Holy Book: The Koran

For twenty-two years, Muhammad recited, and the result is one of the most significant books of mankind, the Koran (which means "The Recitation"). Made up of 114 "Recitations" (or chapters called Suras), the Koran crystallized the Arab language and spread it across much of the world. The Koran is a visionary's book, passionately conveying Muhammad's genius and intuition.

Central Teaching: The Five Pillars

The word *Islam* means "submission" in Arabic. A Muslim is a "submitted one." The focus of Islam is submission to Allah, and the central teaching of Islam is that the "way of submission" involves faithfully practicing Five Pillars:

1. *Recite the shahada.* The *shahada* is Islam's central confession: "There is no god but Allah, and Muhammad is his prophet."

2. *Pray [salat] five times a day facing Mecca.* Faithful Muslims must pray each day at sunrise, noon, midafternoon, sunset, and early evening.

3. *Give [zakat] alms to the poor.* Muslims are to give 2.5 percent of their income. *Zakat* includes giving from any plunder received by defeating an enemy.

4. *Fast [sawm] during the month of Ramadan.* The faithful must refrain from eating, drinking, smoking, and sexual activity during the daylight hours of this holy month. Ramadan is the ninth month of the Muslim calendar, believed to be the month in which the Koran was originally revealed.

5. *Perform a pilgrimage [hajj] to Mecca at least once.* While in Mecca, certain sites must be visited and rituals performed. This pillar may be waived if the participant cannot afford the trip.

Muhammad's Life

Muhammad's new teaching caused strained relations in his home city of Mecca. In 622, when the leaders of his tribe turned against him, Muhammad and his followers relocated to the oasis of Yathrib, 250 miles north of Mecca. This famous journey is known as the *Hijra*, or emigration. Yathrib was renamed Medina ("the City") and is the cradle of the Islamic faith.

Muhammad conducted seven raids on merchant caravans traveling to Mecca over the next eighteen months,[92] solidifying his position and power. In 624, he expelled the Jewish Qainuqa tribe from Medina and divided their properties among his followers. The following year, he did the same to the Nadir, a second Jewish tribe in the city. In the spring of 627, he charged the city's third Jewish tribe (the Qurayza) with collaboration with the enemy, beheaded the six to eight hundred men of the tribe, and sold their women and children into slavery. Muhammad brought the surrounding Bedouin tribes under his influence and continued to increase in power until, in 630, Mecca capitulated to him.

On June 8, 632, the prophet died in the house of his favorite wife, A'isha. At the time of his death, Islamic power extended throughout most of the Arabian peninsula. Muhammad taught his followers, "Believers, make war on the infidels who dwell around you. Deal firmly with them. Know that God is with the righteous" (Sura 9:123). In an impressive wave of victories, Muslim troops conquered all of North Africa to the Atlantic, Spain, most of Asia Minor, Iraq, Iran, and parts of India to the borders of China over the next one hundred years.[93]

View of the Afterlife: Paradise

Muslims believe that faithfully performing the Five Pillars of the faith will earn them entrance into Paradise. Paradise is a place of celebration and happiness. The Koran pictures it this way:

> They shall recline on couches lined with thick brocade, and within reach will hang the fruits of both gardens. Which of the Lord's blessings would you deny? Therein are bashful virgins whom neither man nor jinnee will have touched before. Which of your Lord's blessings would you deny? Virgins as fair as coral and rubies. (Sura 55:54–60)

The *jinn* are a class of beings mentioned often in the Koran. According to Islamic texts, they inhabit an unseen world that is beyond our universe. They are not angels but, along with angels and humans, are one of the three wise and intelligent creations of God.

Another portrayal of Paradise comes in Sura 56:

> *They shall recline on jeweled couches face to face, and there shall wait on them immortal youths with bowls and ewers and a cup of purest wine (that will neither pain their heads nor take away their reason); with fruits of their own choice and flesh of fowls that they will relish. And theirs shall be the dark-eyed houris, chaste as hidden pearls: a guerdon [reward] for their deeds. (Sura 56:15–25)*

Houri is Arabic for "gazelle-eyed." Sura 56:35–37 describes them as "most refined," created by Allah "in the best of form," "virgin, loving, and well-matched."

Islam in Comparison to Christianity

Islam and Christianity are both proselytizing religions. Muhammad commissioned his followers to bring the world into "Dar Islam" (the house of Islam). Christ commissioned His followers to *"Go and make disciples of all nations"* (Matthew 28:19).

Muhammad's methodology for bringing the world to Allah is strikingly different than Jesus's method for bringing the world to Himself. Muslims are commissioned to conquer the world by the sword, where Christians are commanded to proclaim the Good News of Jesus to the ends of the earth. Islam looks forward to a day when the whole world will recite, "There is no god but Allah, and Muhammad is his prophet,"[94] while Christianity looks for a day when *"This gospel of the kingdom will be preached in the whole world as a testimony to all nations"* (Matthew 24:14).

CHAPTER 17

WHAT DO HINDUS BELIEVE?

Just as people are destined to die once, and after that to face judgment, so Christ was sacrificed once to take away the sins of many; and he will appear a second time, not to bear sin, but to bring salvation to those who are waiting for him.

—Hebrews 9:27–28

Hinduism teaches an eternity of lifetimes followed by Moksha, which is a release from the cycle of deaths and rebirths into a complete state of self-realization. Moksha means "emancipate" or "liberate." Hinduism has roughly a billion followers today. The word *Hindu* is Persian for "Indian." Seventy percent of the nation of India follows the Hindu religion.

View of God: Pantheism

According to Hindu teaching, Brahman is the universal spirit, which is everywhere and in everything. It is the unconscious, impersonal force that governs the universe. Hinduism is a pantheistic religion. *Pan* is the Latin word for "all." Hindus believe that God is in everything. Brahman is the great force, the circle of life that ordains everything and puts everything in its place.

Holy Book: The Vedas

Over the centuries, Hindu holy men have recorded their thoughts on how to get along in this world and the next. Hindus hold these writings as sacred. The main Hindu holy books are the Vedas (there are four of them) and the Upanishads (a series of elaborations on the Vedas).

Central Teaching: Reincarnation

Hinduism dates back to 3000 BC. As ancient Hindus looked around their landscape, they noticed a certain hierarchy to our world. The fish eats the worm, the cat eats the fish, the coyote eats the cat, the mountain lion eats the coyote, the mountain lion gets captured by the game warden and transported to a safer place so that he won't eat the game warden's children. They also noted that even this hierarchy tends to go through a predictable cycle: The game warden dies, is buried in the ground, worms eat his body, and the whole thing begins over again. From this, Hindus developed their concept of the road to heaven called "the transmigration of souls," or reincarnation. They believe that all life has an animating force that inhabits certain physical forms based on its level of goodness, as earned in previous lives. This is called "karma."

Here's an example from one of Hinduism's sacred writings:

> *The murderer of a Brahman becomes consumptive, the killer of a cow becomes bump-backed and imbecile, the murderer of a virgin becomes leprous—all three born as outcasts. The slayer of a woman and the destroyer of embryos becomes a savage full of diseases; who commits illicit intercourse, a eunuch; who goes with his teacher's wife, disease-skinned.*

The eater of flesh becomes very red; the drinker of intoxicants, one with discoloured teeth. . . . Who steals food becomes a rat; who steals grain becomes a locust. . . . Perfumes, a musk-rat; honey, a gad-fly; flesh, a vulture; and salt, an ant. . . .

Who commits unnatural vice becomes a village pig; who consorts with a Sudra woman becomes a bull; who is passionate becomes a lustful horse. . . .

These and other signs and births . . . are seen to be the karma of the embodied, made by themselves in this world. Thus the makers of bad karma, having experienced the tortures of hell, are born with the residues of their sins, in these stated forms. (Garuda Purana 5)

In the twentieth century, Indian gurus began emigrating to the United States and presenting their teachings on reincarnation. Upwardly mobile, optimistic Americans didn't like the idea that we could regress in our development. The American dream is about more, never less. So when Hinduism came to America, we modified the transmigrational highway, making it run only one way—up. This belief system became known as the "New Age Movement." The New Age Movement believes in reincarnation, but never in a downward direction. New Age teachers proclaim that we are all gods and that the god-part of us can't go backward, only forward. This belief in purely upward mobility is sometimes called "Cosmic Optimism."

The goal of every Hindu is to live a life that merits good karma. This will enable them to progress forward on the transmigrational highway to a higher level of existence in their next life here on earth. If they do this well enough, over time they will advance to the highest level of humanity, which is the caste of Hindu priest called Brahman. If a Brahman stores up enough karma, eventually he will be elevated out of physical existence into a state of semi-godhood, becoming a spirit. If he progresses forward, life after life in that spirit life, he'll be able to advance to the next higher spirit life.

"Just as the body casts off worn-out clothes and puts on new ones, so the infinite, immortal self casts off worn-out bodies and enters into new ones." Krishna, The Bhagavad-Gita 2:22

View of the Afterlife: Moksha

The ultimate goal of a Hindu is to become pure spirit, completely one with the Brahman of the universe. Achieving this state is sometimes called "Nirvana," which literally means "blown away." Because the Hindus' god is an impersonal force that inhabits all things, when people achieve Nirvana they lose all sense of consciousness and become absorbed into the unconsciousness of the universe. Hence, the pathway to Nirvana (or Moksha) involves multiple lifetimes of living well, dying well, and being born again. Hindu scholars estimate that it takes roughly 600,000 lifetimes to reach the perfect release of Moksha.

Hinduism in Comparison to Christianity

The Bible mentions only eight people coming back from the dead. The prophets Elijah[95] and Elisha[96] each raised one, as did the Apostle Peter[97] and the Apostle Paul.[98] Three more were raised by Jesus,[99] and the eighth was Jesus Christ Himself. The Bible teaches that everyone else has only one earthly life, as explained in Hebrews 9:27–28: *"Just as people are destined to die once, and after that to face judgment, so Christ was sacrificed once to take away the sins of many; and he will appear a second time, not to bear sin, but to bring salvation to those who are waiting for him."*

CHAPTER 18

WHAT DO BUDDHISTS BELIEVE?

Therefore, since Christ suffered in his body, arm yourselves also with the same attitude, because whoever suffers in the body is done with sin. As a result, they do not live the rest of their earthly lives for evil human desires, but rather for the will of God.

—1 Peter 4:1–2

Buddhism has just shy of 500 million adherents, which equates to about 6 percent of the world's population. Its founder, Siddhartha Gautama, was born in approximately 563 BC to a high caste Hindu family in Nepal. At about the age of forty, Gautama concluded that Hinduism was an inadequate system of belief.

He meditated under a fig tree for forty days and nights to consider the matter. During this meditation, he became "enlightened" about the nature of life and the means to eternity. For the next fifty years, he was known as "the Buddha," which means "the Enlightened One."

View of God: "A Noble Silence"

According to Buddhism, God is beyond description. A leading Buddhist scholar explained,

The Buddhist teaching on God, in the sense of an ultimate Reality, is neither agnostic, as is sometimes claimed, nor vague, but clear and logical. Whatever Reality may be, it is beyond the conception of the finite intellect; it follows that attempts at description are misleading, unprofitable, and a waste of time. For these good reasons, the Buddha maintained about Reality, "a noble silence."[100]

Central Teachings: The Four Noble Truths and the Eightfold Path

During his meditation, the Buddha discovered the Four Noble Truths. These truths explain the reality of life.

1. *Suffering is universal.* The very act of living brings about pain and suffering. If you are human, you will suffer.

2. *Craving is the root cause of suffering.* If we didn't desire things, we wouldn't feel deprived or lacking or that our lives weren't exactly what we want them to be.

3. *The cure for suffering is to eliminate craving.* If we can emotionally detach ourselves from desires, then what once felt like a deprivation no longer feels so.

4. *Craving is eliminated by following the Eightfold Path.* Following the Eightfold Path enables one to rise above and become enlightened.

The Eightfold Path involves the following:

1. *Right views* (right understanding of the Four Noble Truths)

2. *Right thought* (about truth)

3. *Right speech* (no lying, no slander, no cruel words)

4. *Right behavior* (no killing any living creatures, no stealing, no sexual misconduct)

5. *Right occupation* (seek gainful employment)

6. *Right effort* (to attain enlightenment, strive to rid yourself of all your bad qualities, seek human perfection)

7. *Right contemplation* (be alert and observant of all that's going on around you in this life)

8. *Right meditation* (to enter enlightenment)

The ultimate goal of Buddhism is to be free from pain and suffering. By following his Eightfold Path, the Buddha taught that a person could achieve "enlightenment." Buddhism teaches, "Those who love a hundred have a hundred woes. Those who love ten have ten woes. Those who love one have one woe. Those who love none have no woes."[101] So Buddhism does not focus much on the afterlife, but on this life and the way to overcome suffering, which is to detach yourself from it.

View of the Afterlife: Nirvana

Like the Hinduism from which it sprang, Buddhism believes in Nirvana, but with a slight twist. Because Buddha saw all life and life-forms as temporary, there is no "ultimate place."

> *Traditional [Buddhist] teaching is that there are six realms of existence into which one can be reborn: as a hell being, a "hungry" ghost, an animal, a human being, a jealous god and*

a heavenly being. The most precious of these is seen to be the human birth as this gives the best opportunities for winning enlightenment. A heavenly being is too absorbed in pleasure to think about winning enlightenment. Unlike Christianity, Buddhism sees these states as ultimately temporary. A god, therefore, will eventually descend into one of the lower realms.[102]

For a Buddhist, the ultimate destination of the soul is fluid; it changes from one life to the next. The path to enlightenment is through disengagement from the cares of this world. If God exists, He or it is an impersonal force best not discussed since we cannot adequately describe Him.

"Man is born alone, lives alone and dies alone, and it is he alone who can blaze the way which leads him to Nirvana." Buddha

---

Buddhism in Comparison to Christianity

Christianity takes a far different view of suffering and detachment. It says that suffering is profitable in many ways. According to the Bible, Jesus Christ, God's Son, didn't avoid suffering; He deliberately chose to experience it on behalf of mankind. Jesus told His followers in Luke 9:22, *"The Son of Man must suffer many things and be rejected by the elders . . . and he must be killed and on the third day be raised to life."*

Hebrews 2:18 says, *"Because he himself suffered when he was tempted, he is able to help those who are being tempted."* In Hebrews 4:15, it says that because Jesus suffered, He is able to *"empathize with our weaknesses."* Furthermore, Hebrews 5:8 says that Christ *"learned obedience from what he suffered."*

Hebrews 12:7 teaches Christ's followers to *"endure hardship as discipline,"* because going through hardship builds character. Romans 5:3–4 explains that *"suffering produces perseverance; perseverance, character; and character, hope."* Elsewhere, 2 Corinthians 1:4 explains that suffering enables Christ followers to *"comfort those in any trouble with the comfort we ourselves receive from God."*

The Apostle Paul in 2 Timothy 2:3 went so far as to encourage his friends to *"join with me in suffering, like a good soldier of Christ Jesus,"* and in 2 Timothy 1:8 to *"join with me in suffering for the gospel,"* so that others would be able to hear and understand God's message of love for them.

In this way, Christianity is the antithesis of Buddhism. Christ entered into the sufferings of the world in order to help the world. He taught His disciples to do the same. Buddha attempted to detach himself from his sufferings and the sufferings of the world, and he taught his disciples to do likewise. As twentieth-century mathematician and philosopher Alfred North Whitehead said, "The Buddha gave his doctrine; Christ gave his life."

CHAPTER 19

WHAT DO CHRISTIANS BELIEVE?

For it is by grace you have been saved, through faith—and this is not from yourselves, it is the gift of God—not by works, so that no one can boast.

—Ephesians 2:8-9

Christianity's founder, Jesus Christ, was born in Bethlehem, probably around 4 BC. At age thirty, Jesus began to heal, teach, and perform miracles while preparing His disciples to carry on His ministry. In April of AD 29, He was crucified, buried, and resurrected from the grave.[103] For forty days He appeared to people before ascending into heaven.[104]

Ten days later, the Holy Spirit descended on Jesus's followers, empowering them to preach, heal, and perform miracles.[105] With 2.2 billion adherents, Christianity is the largest religion on earth. It is estimated that more than 100,000 people become Christians each day.[106]

View of God: Monotheism

Christianity teaches that God is one Person manifesting Himself in three personalities (Father, Son, and Holy Spirit). This is illustrated in Genesis 1, where God the Father *speaks* creation into existence while the Spirit is present. "Speaks" is a reference to the second person of the Trinity, called *"the Word"* in John

1:1. Father, Son, and Holy Spirit were all present at Creation. He's a God in community with Himself. This is confirmed at the end in Genesis 1:26 where, instead of saying, "*I am going to make people in my image,*" He says, "*Let us make mankind in our image.*" Thus God, who is in community, wanted to extend that community, so He created people like Himself. One of Christianity's central teachings is that men and women were created to have a relationship with God.

"There are many religions in the world, but only one Christianity, for only Christianity has a God who gave Himself for mankind. World religions attempt to reach up to God; Christianity is God reaching down to man." Billy Graham

---

Central Teaching: Grace

On the night before His crucifixion, Jesus said, "*If I go and prepare a place for you, I will come back and take you to be with me that you also may be where I am*" (John 14:3). God wants us to be with Him. The dilemma of mankind is that we are separated from God because of our sin (our moral shortcomings). Every culture in every age has had a belief in God and a desire to be united with Him in some way. Christianity's solution to God and men getting together is called *grace.*

Hebrews 9:22 says, "*Without the shedding of blood there is no forgiveness.*" In Exodus 12, God introduced the idea of a sin substitute when He asked the Israelites to sacrifice an unblemished lamb on behalf of the family's sins. Presumed in this is the concept of justice. Justice demands payment when a wrong has occurred. Everyone wants justice. We don't want to live in a world where God treats Saddam Hussein and Mother Teresa alike. We want things to be fair.

God wants justice too. But, because He is completely loving, He wants more than justice. He wants to extend mercy. How can He be merciful while maintaining justice? God's solution was (and is) substitution. To maintain a just world, God demands payment for wrongdoing. To keep us from paying that price (which would mean eternal separation from Him), He stepped down from heaven and paid the price Himself. That's grace. The Bible describes it this way: *"When the kindness and love of God our Savior appeared, he saved us, not because of righteous things we had done, but because of his mercy"* (Titus 3:4–5).

Four Solutions

In Genesis 3, Adam and Eve ate the forbidden fruit, and their sin caused separation from God. For the next eight chapters, God did something very creative: Before He gave the *substitution solution*, He demonstrated the futility of the solutions that each of the other three major religions would eventually devise.

1. The Isolation Solution

In Genesis 4, God demonstrated the *isolation solution*. Cain and Abel brought offerings to God. Because Cain failed to bring the firstfruits of his crops, God said in effect, "You can do better than that." In frustration, Cain lashed out and killed his brother. God said, "Cain, from now on, you are going to live in isolation from the rest of the community." He banished Cain from the rest of humanity so that he wouldn't hurt or be hurt by them.

This is the Buddhist solution: Withdraw yourself. If you can't be touched, you can't be hurt. This solution didn't work for Cain. He cried out, *"My punishment is more than I can bear"* (Genesis 4:13).

2. The Repetition Solution

God demonstrated the second solution, the *repetition solution*, in Genesis 6. Because people were doing things to each other that were so hurtful, God caused a great flood to eliminate all mankind, except the family of Noah. He then started humanity over again with this one ideal family.

This is the solution of Hinduism. With enough reincarnations, eventually you will accumulate enough good karma to get close to God. The problem? No matter how many chances we get, we're still flawed and finite people, so we remain imperfect and fall short. This solution didn't work for Noah. Not long after his children stepped off the boat, they got into a family feud. Noah got drunk, one of his sons ridiculed him, and Noah cursed that son and all his descendants.[107]

3. The Exertion Solution

In Genesis 11, people got together and tried to work their way back to God. They built a tower stretching toward the sky. Their plan was to work hard enough to earn their way to heaven. The *exertion solution* is by far the most common response to the problem of aloneness. Islam says, "Practice the Five Pillars. Given enough effort, you'll earn your way to Paradise." The Mormons, Jehovah's Witnesses, and dozens of other smaller religions have adopted strategies for earning their way to God as well.

4. The Relational Solution

After God got through demonstrating the inadequacies of these methods, He began to put His own solution into place. His solution is a relationship based on grace. In Genesis 12, God chose one man, Abram (soon to be renamed Abraham), built a relationship with him, and began to teach him about grace.

God promised that He would turn Abraham into a great nation that would bless *"all peoples on earth"* (Genesis 12:3).

In Exodus 12, God introduced the nation of Israel to the idea of simultaneously fulfilling justice and giving mercy by providing a substitute payment for the people's sins. God said to Moses,

> *Tell the whole community of Israel that on the tenth day of this month each man is to take a lamb for his family. . . . The animals you choose must be year-old males without defect. . . . Take care of them until the fourteenth day of the month, when all the members of the community of Israel must slaughter them at twilight.* (Exodus 12:3, 5–6)

The lamb served as the grace solution for the people. The forfeit of its life served as payment for sin, allowing God to maintain justice while giving grace.

This idea reached its fulfillment in Jesus Christ. On the day Christ began His ministry, John the Baptist declared, *"Look, the Lamb of God, who takes away the sin of the world!"* (John 1:29). For the next three years, Jesus proclaimed that the kingdom of God was at hand. At the end of that time, He was led up a hill to His death, like an innocent lamb to the slaughter. After several hours on the cross, Jesus looked up to heaven and said, *"It is finished"* (John 19:30). This was God's solution to man's separation from Him: He enforced justice by taking a life, but the life He took was the life of His Son. God grants forgiveness based on the merits of another.

The Bible says, *"To all who did receive him, to those who believed in his name, he gave the right to become children of God"* (John 1:12). In Christianity, instead of asking us to make the effort, God makes the effort for us.

This means that every person in the world is only one prayer away from heaven. The prayer is a simple request: *"Lord, thank You for what Christ did for me on the cross. Please accept His sin payment on my behalf, and come live Your life as my Lord."*

View of the Afterlife: Heaven

The Bible describes heaven as a place in God's presence where *"there will be no more death or mourning or crying or pain"* (Revelation 21:4). Entrance is granted based on knowing Christ. People from every culture and language will be there.[108] And everyone will be given responsibilities commensurate with those they assumed for Christ here on earth.[109] We'll cover this in detail during the chapters on Question #5.

CHAPTER 20

WHAT DO THE OTHER RELIGIONS BELIEVE?

Choose for yourselves this day whom you will serve, whether the gods your ancestors served beyond the Euphrates, or the gods of the Amorites, in whose land you are living. But as for me and my household, we will serve the Lord.

—Joshua 24:15

In recent years, sociologists have studied and cataloged every religious system that has ten thousand or more followers. The following chart displays the largest of these religions, along with each one's percentage of followers.[110]

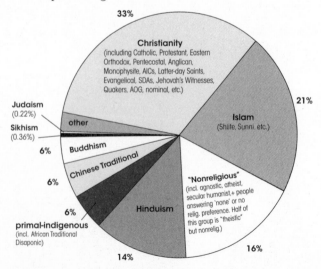

NOTE: Total adds up to more than 100% due to rounding and because upper bound estimates were used for each group.

©2005 www.adherents.com

You may be surprised to learn that there are very few truly viable religions. Ninety seven percent of the world adheres to one of only seven faith systems. Increase this number to the top ten religions, and you'll include 98 percent of humanity.

What about the other hundreds of religions practiced around the world? Their adherence numbers are so small that if any one of them is right, then more than 99.8 percent of us are wrong. Admittedly, perhaps *all* religions are wrong, but if there is one right religion, surely we will find it among the top ten. Let's explore them from smallest to largest:

#10—Juche
Followers = 19 million North Koreans (.03%)
Founder = Kim Il-sung, 1950s

Juche, also known as Kimilsungism, is the national religion of North Korea. It was created and mandated by Kim Il-sung, North Korea's first communist dictator, soon after he came to power in the 1950s. Jucheism has nineteen million adherents because North Korea has nineteen million inhabitants. It is the only government-sanctioned ideology; every other religion is outlawed. *Juche* means "self-reliance" in Korean. Its promoters describe it as a secular, ethical philosophy and not a religion. From a sociological viewpoint, Juche is a Korean blending of Marxist-Communist thought. It makes no claims about heaven and generates no belief that life after death might or might not exist.

"All religions do not teach the same thing but differ at key points." R. C. Sproul

---

#9—Sikhism
Followers = 23 million, chiefly in Punjab, India (.038%)
Founder = Guru Nanak, AD 1469
View of God = Monotheism
Means to God = The Five Ks

The Sikh religion is a blending of Hinduism and Islam. Its founder was Guru Nanak Dev, born in 1469, who endured years of violence between the Muslims and the Hindus in his area. Nanak's solution to the problem of the war was to adopt the concept of monotheism from the Muslims and the concepts of karma and reincarnation from the Hindus. The revelation he taught was, "There is no Hindu, no Muslim."

There are twenty-three million Sikhs, most of them living in the Indian state of Punjab, though some have emigrated to the United Kingdom, Canada, the United States, Malaysia, and Singapore. The Sikhs are monotheists. In order to escape the endless wandering of the soul that happens as reincarnation follows reincarnation, a devout Sikh must carry certain articles of faith at all times. They are known as "the Five Ks" and are worn to identify and represent Sikhism's ideals:

1. *Kesh*: "uncut hair" for honesty

2. *Kanga*: "wooden comb" for equality

3. *Kara*: "metal bracelet" for meditation

4. *Kachera*: "specially designed underwear" for fidelity

5. *Kirpan*: "strapped sword" for never bowing to tyranny

Sikhs make up 10 to 15 percent of the Indian army and 20 percent of its officers, which makes them ten times more likely to be a soldier and officer in the Indian army than the average

Indian. Because of the turbans they customarily wear, many Westerners mistake Sikhs for Muslims or even terrorists, which has resulted in an increase of hate crimes against Sikhs in the United States and Britain since the events of 9/11.

#8—African Traditional Religion
Followers = 95 million in Africa and places where Africans were enslaved (1.6%)
View of God = Polytheism
Means to God = Sacrifices

This religion is actually a large grouping of religions. Among its various tribes and adaptations, there are approximately ninety-five million people who practice this form of animism. *Animism* is the spiritual belief that all creation (plants and animals, rocks and rivers, sand and soil) possesses *animation* or life within it. African traditional religion's view of God is that many gods inhabit every rock and tree, the sky, the moon, and the sun.

Most animistic religions believe that the means to gain favor with the gods is to make sacrifices to them. Pleasing the gods is the key to reaching the afterlife. Many ancient animistic cultures practiced human sacrifice, including the Druids of Northern Europe; the Mayans, Aztecs, and Incas of Latin America; and most of the peoples of the ancient Near East. Modern animists tend to use animals and sometimes flowers or plants as their offerings.

Animists believe in a heaven that is not too different from life on earth. Old American westerns used to feature Native Americans talking about "the Happy Hunting Ground," a spirit world after death where life is similar to, but better than, present human life. The movie *Gladiator* pictures General Maximus Meridius walking through the Elysian Fields after his death. The ancient Greek and Roman pagans believed in this type of afterlife existence.

#7—Primal-Indigenous

Followers = 150 million, including shamans (Siberia), pagans (in Asia and India), and smaller, pre-literate tribal belief systems (2.5%)

This group of religions is comprised of animists who still live on the fringes of literate society. Primal Indigenous peoples' beliefs are similar to African Traditional Religionists, so they all used to be grouped together as simply "animists." But demographers have separated the two groups in recent years out of respect for their distinctive ethnicities.

#6—Chinese Traditional Religions

Followers = 225 million, mostly in China (4%)
Founders = Lao-Tzu (604–531 BC) and Confucius (551–479 BC)
View of God = No particular deity/impersonal force (though Lao-Tzu did become venerated generations later)
Means to God = Not stressed; more of an ethical system than a religious one

As the name implies, most of Chinese Traditional Religionists live in China. Lao-Tzu founded Taoism, and Confucius founded Confucianism. Both are chiefly concerned with how to live an honorable life by treating people well and venerating one's ancestors. None of the major branches of this group concern themselves much with God or the afterlife. Chinese Traditional Religions have more of a here-and-now focus.

#5—Buddhism

Followers = 488 million
Founder = Siddhartha Guatama (563–483 BC)
View of God = Not stressed
Means to God = The Four Noble Truths

Like Chinese Traditional Religionists, Buddha focused on how to live here and now. As we discussed earlier, most branches of Buddhism do not stress or describe God or an afterlife.

Followers = 850 million, nonreligious Westerners, agnostics, and atheists in current and former communist countries (14%)

Scholars lump these groups together because they all purport a lack of interest in religion or spirituality. But one observer noted,

> Sociologists point out that there are no truly "secular" societies. . . . "Nonreligious" people . . . are those who derive their worldview and value system from alternative, secular, cultural or otherwise nonrevealed systems rather than traditional religious systems.[111]

Some, like Michael Newdow who was mentioned in chapter 6, would say, "I don't really know what I believe. And it doesn't really matter." Many have made the conscious choice not to explore their faith, or at least not to do so publicly.

#3—Hinduism

Followers = 1 billion	
Founded = 1800–1000 BC	
View of God = Pantheism, Universal life force	
Means to God = Transmigrational highway	
View of Afterlife = Nirvana	

#2—Islam

Followers = 1.6 billion	
Founder = Muhammad, AD 610	
View of God = Monotheism	
Means to God = The Five Pillars of Islam	
View of Afterlife = Paradise	

#1—Christianity
Followers = 2.2 billion
Founder = Jesus Christ, AD 33
View of God = Monotheism (Trinitarianism)
Means to God = Atonement/Substitution
View of Afterlife = Heaven

Some Observations

Every religion claims to be the only way to God. Every religion has a different road, and almost all the roads purport to lead to different places. To help you make a choice, try answering these questions: Which of these systems matches the description of how life seems to work on earth? Which of them offers the most believable description of God? Which of them matches what my heart tells me is true?

CHAPTER 21

HOW DO I TALK TO PEOPLE WHO HOLD OTHER RELIGIOUS BELIEFS?

I am God, and there is no other;
I am God, and there is none like me.

—Isaiah 46:9

We all have friends who say "The world's religions are all basically the same." If you've read this far, you know all religions are not the same. There are a few overlaps, but not much agreement on the existence of God, the nature of God, the nature of the afterlife, or how one gets there.

Without thinking much about it, most modern people lump all belief systems into the "religion" basket and leave it there, pigeon-holing each one as culturally different perspectives of the same God. Particularly in the West, we've bred the value of religious tolerance into our popular thinking, not from a realistic exploration of the Coexist religions of the world. That approach has produced the movement that says "All religions are the same so lets just get along."

The Problem of Reducing

Ideas about the spiritual world can't be reduced to one broad, inclusive system. They're too different and unique. And each one's adherents feels too strongly to let people erase what they believe are critical components of their core beliefs. Each major world religion has a differing perspective.

Since you've traveled with us on this brief tour of the major religions, you should see how unique Christianity is. Other religions are "do" religions and Christianity is "done." All the other religions require their followers to "do" certain pious exercises to earn approval from God or the universe. Jesus came to bring us to the Father through His redemptive work on the cross. The work to make us acceptable doesn't fall on our shoulders. It's already been "done" through the work of Jesus. That is why He says:

"I am the way and the truth and the life. No one comes to the Father except through me."
—John 14:6

Postmodern thinking looks at John 14:6 and concludes that Jesus and his followers are narrow-minded and intolerant of other religions. Instead, we just know Jesus has paved a way for us to come to the Father without requiring us acts or efforts or struggles to become perfect. Jesus already made the way for us.

The Problem of Exclusivity

Today's broadminded value of tolerance struggles with the idea of "exclusive truth." But let's clarify: Jesus isn't saying other paths don't lead somewhere. Every path leads somewhere. He's just saying "If you want to come to the Father, I've made the way for you."

Someone could say, "I believe that all roads lead to California." But we know that can't true. Believing can't change physical reality. All roads will not take you to California.

Jesus' statement in John 14:6 is not negative, it's positive. He lovingly invites us to know the Father and announces that He wants to take us to the Father because we are unable to get there on our own moral merit. Jesus didn't say all religions must be destroyed, or proven wrong. He just invites us to life in the Father and He shares how awesome that can be.

He shared in an earlier passage that the Father is Spirit and those who worship Him must do so in Spirit and truth. Jesus is not selfish or exclusive. He invites everyone to know His Father. He did not create separation, He built a bridge. He never drew lines to keep out those who were irreligious.

We have provided you with information on how the primary world religions operate so you can draw your own conclusions.

Practical Conversations

You might be wondering how to engage a friend in conversation about these things. Here's what we recommend: understand the basic tenets of your own faith, then, just share what you've learned here as you've read about the other religions of the world. Your friend will respect the effort you've put into understanding others' religious beliefs.

As you discuss your journey, your friend may be moved by the power of the gospel.

Your conversation might go like this:

"I've been surveying the world's religions. Tell me about yours. I would be fascinated to learn more about... Hinduism, Islam or Judaism etc."

You're willingness to listen just might increase their openness to listening to the good news of Jesus.

This is what I call an "innocent awe" approach. Think about the innocence of a child. Children are masters at being open and receptive. I don't know exactly when it happens, but we tend to grow cynical and skeptical as we get more "worldly wise." We lose our amazement, curiosity and astonishment at the wonders that surround us.

Innocent Awe

How is it that children are able to ask penetrating and thought provoking questions? They haven't developed social filters yet, nor learned to practice the feigned interest of adulthood.

How many times have you been surprised by a child's simple insights? I am amazed daily at the insightful things children say. They see the world for what it is, they have not become jaded. That age of innocence allows them to winsomely connect with others in ways adults have long since forgotten.

You can learn to ask innocent questions like a child, combined with the social and relational skills of an adult. Employing innocent awe, you can approach friends with a humble heart, like a child. Jesus said, "Whoever humbles himself like a child is the greatest in the Kingdom" (Matthew 18:4, ESV).

Try it. Practicing innocent awe can open up powerful spiritual conversations. And when people begin asking and seeking, they start the process that leads them to the Father.

Open, innocent questions make you a friend, not an adversary. With your help, your friend will be able to ask themselves open and innocent questions. Given time, open asking leads to finding the Truth.

And asking leads to reciprocity. You ask me a sincere personal question, I'm naturally going to reciprocate by asking you one in return. When your friend asks, "And why do you believe what you believe," well, that can get exciting to the point of life-changing!

Nobody Likes a Know-It-All

In the past, I have fallen prey to the false belief that I must be the answer person. It is better simply to engage people and listen to their story. As long as you think you have to have all the answers, you're going turn people off. Jesus was constantly asking questions. He knew that every question has the potential to open up a conversation that can point someone to the Father.

Fight the temptation to be a biblical know-it-all.

The Bible says that when we share with someone the hope that we have, we must do it in a gentle and respectful way.

"Be prepared to give an answer to everyone who asks you to give the reason for the hope that you have. But do this with gentleness and respect." —1 Peter 3:15

HOW CAN A GOOD GOD ALLOW SUFFERING?

CHAPTER 22

WHAT ARE THE POSSIBILITIES?

Are you still maintaining your integrity? Curse God and die!
—Job 2:9

I (Hal) gave the members of my church an assignment: Ask your neighbors, "If you could ask God any question, what would you like to know?" The "Why is there suffering?" question won hands down. "If God is all-knowing, then He is aware of everything that goes on. If He is all-powerful, then He can prevent or correct anything bad. And if He is all-loving, then He cares about everything that goes on. So, why do so many bad things happen in our world?"

Because the world contains so much sorrow and evil, some people conclude that God cannot be all-knowing, all-powerful, and all-loving at the same time. He can be two out of three, but if He were all three, He could not possibly sit back and allow the tragedies that occur on our planet on a daily basis. Or could He? Let's look at some of the ways different groups have answered the question of suffering.

A Two-out-of-Three God

Maybe the reason suffering exists in the world is because God is all-knowing and all-powerful but isn't very loving. If this is true, suffering exists because God doesn't care enough to do anything about it. He's at best disinterested, and at worst delighted with the pain and hurt He sees inflicted on people and the planet.

A second possibility is that God is all-powerful and all-loving but lacks the ability to know and see everything that is going on, so evil and suffering often slip by Him.

"Pain is weakness leaving the body."
U.S. Marines T-shirt

The third possibility is that God is all-knowing and all-loving but lacks power. He's too weak to prevent evil from happening.

Option #1 leaves us with a scary God, a God who knows about everything and is strong enough to do anything. He is un-restrained. No compassion or morals keep Him from torturing His creation. He can change the rules, both moral and physical, anytime He wishes. Tomorrow morning we might wake up to find that gravity no longer holds or that photosynthesis doesn't work or that justice is no longer a virtue but has become a vice.

Option #2 gives us a blind God. This God is strong and loving but slow because He can't foresee, or merely see, what is presently going on with us. This God wants to help; it just takes Him a while.

Option #3 delivers a sissy God. He sees everything and wants to help; He just can't. He's not strong enough.

All three of these options are flawed. God #1 is warped. None of us goes to bed worried that the sun won't rise or that water will suddenly begin running uphill. The universe appears to have a constancy and predictability to it that testifies to a strong, wise, and loving divinity.

God #2 is illogical. If the only reason evil keeps breaking out is because God can't see it coming or doesn't notice it tak-ing place, why wouldn't this God, who created time, do a little rewinding and set it all right the second time around?

God #3 is ridiculous. This God is either an aging grandfather who once was able to do mighty things or a custodial God who *was always* too weak to govern and control nature. He's just sitting in for someone stronger who, apparently, has left the scene.

Another Approach: Job and Friends

The book of Job was included in the Bible to help answer the question of suffering. Scholars believe Job may have been written as an ancient drama to be acted out on the stage. Those with major speaking parts are Job, his wife, his friends, and God. Once Job poses the question, "Why is this happening to me?" the remaining characters give answers according to their own understanding.

Answer One: Who's to Blame?

Job's wife gives the first answer. When Job finds that his wealth, health, and children have all been taken from him, she suggests that Job put an end to his misery by putting an end to his life. Her exact words are *"Curse God and die!"* (Job 2:9).

Bitterness and blame are often the reactions of people in or near suffering. In the face of such seeming unfairness, many would go so far as to conclude God doesn't exist. Funny thing, though: Most people who conclude that there isn't a God still blame that nonexistent God for the problems in the universe. They've stopped believing, but they haven't stopped blaming.

If God doesn't exist, then where did we ever get the notion that life should be fair in the first place? Where did that sense of justice come from?

Answer Two: So It's My Fault

Job's friends give a second answer. As Eliphaz, Bildad, and Zophar sit down with Job and watch him pick scabs, they listen and lament with him. After listening for several days, they've had enough and start giving advice. The three friends say things like, "*Consider now: Who, being innocent, has ever perished?*" (Job 4:7). And "*All his days the wicked man suffers torment*" (Job 15:20). And "*The mirth of the wicked is brief, the joy of the godless lasts but a moment*" (Job 20:5). For all their initial compassion, these friends are now saying, "Face it, Job, you sinned. That's why you're suffering." It's the moralist answer to evil: The world has a balance to it, and you only get what you deserve.

Answer Three: God's Perspective

After listening to people's platitudes for almost forty chapters, God brings His own answer to the question. When He does, He rebukes Job's friends for their lack of compassion: "What you're saying is the wrong message, given at the wrong time in the wrong way." When people are in pain, God never responds with a platitude. (At the end of the book of Job, God even tells these friends, "You owe Job an apology.") From chapters 38 to 41, God answers Job in a way that puts the question into per-spective—God's perspective.

Only when we see the problem of pain from the perspec-tive of God can we hope to find a true, whole, sense-making answer. Toward the close of the book, as Job raises his voice and demands an explanation from God, God answers him, "Job, where were you when I hung the constellations? Can you explain where light comes from? Or how darkness came into being? Can you understand the miracle of how conception takes place?"

God's answer to Job when he asks "Why?" is not about suf-fering; it's about Job himself. God reminds Job of who is God and who is not. It's not a very satisfying answer to me, but it is to Job. After God speaks, Job says, "*Surely I spoke of things I did not*

understand, things too wonderful for me to know. . . . Therefore I
despise myself and repent in dust and ashes" (Job 42:3, 6).

But I Want an Explanation!

I have thought about this for a while, and it occurs to me that when calamity strikes someone I love, I want an explanation. But when calamity strikes me, I want comfort. God doesn't owe Job an explanation. He doesn't really owe you or me one, either. Besides, if He really is God, 99.9 percent of the explanation would be over our heads anyway. Frederick Buechner said, "For God to try to explain the kinds of things Job wants explained would be like Einstein explaining relativity to a little-neck clam." I like the way author Philip Yancey put it: "Maybe sometimes God keeps us in the dark about 'why' not so much because He wants to keep us in the dark, as because He knows we are incapable of absorbing so much light."

CHAPTER 23

DID GOD CREATE EVIL?

Sighing has become my daily food;
my groans pour out like water.
—Job 3:24

In John 16:33, Jesus made a strange promise. He said, *"In this world you will have trouble."* I'm sure you've experienced this personally and seen it every time you access the news. Our world is indeed full of trouble.

How do you reconcile a good God with a troubled world? Shouldn't He do something about it all? Actually, He is doing something. Something big. He's been working His plan for quite some time. It may just be a little hard to see from your vantage point.

Here's what I mean.

If you have ever tried to start reading a novel at chapter 5 or 6, you know how confusing it can be. The Bible describes the beginning, middle, and ending of history. Right now, we're in the middle of history. The whole thing would make much more sense if we could start at the beginning.

See, in the beginning, God created a paradise. The pinnacle of God's creation was the making of men and women. God made humans with high reasoning capacity and the ability to make choices for themselves. He gave us *free will*. To understand where suffering comes from, you have to understand free will.

The Option for Evil

In order to offer humankind real freedom, God created us with the ability to choose between right and wrong. In the midst of paradise, God designated one tree and said, *"You are free to eat from any tree in the garden; but you must not eat from the tree of the knowledge of good and evil"* (Genesis 2:16–17).

Like a fish that has always lived in water, Adam and Eve knew only one set of circumstances. A fish may live its whole life without experiencing air, which would be a good thing. But the day it leaps above the surface and takes air into its gills, it begins to understand what water really is.

Adam and Eve had no need to know what evil was. But in order for them to have free will, God had to give them the ability to choose between good and evil. At that point, evil was not a reality, only a possibility.

God didn't create evil, but in order to grant us free will, He did create *the potential for evil* by designating the one tree in the Garden of Eden as "off-limits." No one knows how long Adam and Eve lived in the garden before choosing to experience the "off-limits" option. But eventually, they did. Like the fish out of water, from that day forward, they knew what good was because they had experienced its opposite.

A Perfect World

People ask, "Why didn't God create a world where there was no evil and suffering?" Answer: He did.

Genesis 1 spells out God's creation, from land to plants to fish to birds to animals.

Every facet of Creation was good. At the end of His creating, *"God saw all that he had made, and it was very good"* (Genesis 1:31).

So the short answer to the question of evil is, God did not create evil. He created the potential for evil by creating free will.

Evil and suffering are not God's choice. They are the result of the choice made by Adam and Eve. *"When Adam sinned, sin entered the world. Adam's sin brought death, so death spread to everyone, for everyone sinned"* (Romans 5:12, NLT).

"You do not have to sit outside in the dark. If, however, you want to look at the stars, you will find that darkness is required. The stars neither require it nor demand it." Annie Dillard

---

Two Kinds of Evil

Not only do people experience the effects of their sin, creation does as well. Something damaging happened to the physical universe as a result of Adam and Eve's choice. Romans 8:22 says, *"All creation has been groaning as in the pains of childbirth right up to the present time"* (NLT).

This explains natural disasters like earthquakes and hurricanes. When Adam and Eve chose evil, they were telling God they wanted freedom from His sovereignty in their lives. God honored that choice, and nature was cursed. Genetic breakdown and disease began. Pain and death became part of the human experience. Tornadoes, famine, and floods sprang up.

While these "natural" types of calamity occur with regularity, someone has observed that about 95 percent of all suffering comes from what is called *moral evil*. Moral evil is evil inflicted on a person or group by another person or group. When someone dies from a tornado, that's *natural evil*; when someone dies from a stab wound, that's *moral evil*.

Why Would God Let This Happen?

Couples sometimes wrestle with the potential for birth defects and other dangers as they weigh the decision to have children. Most choose to go ahead in spite of the risks.

Why? Because of love. And because of a desire to create something in their own image. And because they want to have a relationship with someone in their own image. God made that same choice.

God created the potential for evil in our world because it was the only way He could create the potential for genuine goodness and genuine love. Humans, freely choosing, brought potential evil to reality.

CHAPTER 24

WHAT'S THE POINT OF PROBLEMS?

*But he knows the way that I take;
when he has tested me, I will come
forth as gold.*

—Job 23:10

Nobody's immune to pain. In the Sermon on the Mount, Jesus said, *"[God] causes his sun to rise on the evil and the good, and sends rain on the righteous and the unrighteous"* (Matthew 5:45). Nobody's immune to sunshine, and nobody's immune to rain.

This may not be great news, but it's not bad news either. It means that whatever hardship I am facing, I'm not the first one to experience it. God hasn't singled me out for cruel and unusual punishment. And if others have gotten through this kind of thing before, chances are I can too. This helps me when I'm in trouble.

Every Problem Has a Purpose

However bad a situation may be, the pain of it is not senseless. Something good can come out of my circumstances if I respond well to them. I'm indebted to Rick Warren for pointing out that the Bible shows five redemptive ways God uses problems in the lives of people.

1. God uses trials to direct me.

Though donkeys have long been used as pack animals, they can be extremely stubborn. When they set their minds to standing still, they will stand there until persuasive force is used. God knows that humans have something in common with the donkey: Sometimes we need to be hit over the head with a two-by-four to get us moving. Proverbs 20:30 says, *"Sometimes it takes a painful experience to make us change our ways"* (GNT). Problems can point us in new directions and motivate us to change.

2. God uses trials to inspect me.

Someone once said, "People are like tea bags; if you want to know what's inside them, drop them in hot water!" James 1:2–3 says, *"When you have many kinds of troubles, you should be full of joy, because you know that these troubles test your faith, and this will give you patience"* (NCV).

3. God uses trials to correct me.

Some lessons can only be learned through pain or failure. Your parents probably told you not to touch a hot stove. But how did you learn not to touch a hot stove? By getting burned! Sometimes we only learn the value of something (like health, money, or a relationship) by losing it. King David said about his pain, *"The punishment you gave me was the best thing that could have happened to me, for it taught me to pay attention to your laws"* (Psalm 119:71, TLB).

4. God uses trials to protect me.

A problem can be a blessing in disguise if it prevents you from being harmed by something more serious. I know a man who lost his job for refusing to do something unethical. His unemployment was a trial, but it may have saved him from jail time a year later when his employer's actions were uncovered.

5. God uses trials to perfect me.

When we respond correctly to trials and troubles, they can become character-builders. Romans 5:3–4 says, *"We can rejoice, too, when we run into problems . . . they help us learn to be patient. And patience develops strength of character in us and helps us trust God more each time we use it until finally our hope and faith are strong and steady"* (TLB).

I usually see the reason for my trials after they are over. In the midst of pain, I'm too numb or too close to diagnose what's happening in me or for me. Understanding almost always comes afterward.

"God whispers to us in our pleasures, He speaks to us in our conscience, but He shouts to us in our pain. It is His megaphone to rouse a deaf world." C. S. Lewis

---

Still, even if I can't figure out what's going on while it's going on, knowing that my suffering can result in good lifts the burden a bit. It's encouraging to know God can use everything, no matter how painful, for my good and His glory.

Life is a series of problem-solving opportunities. Problems will either defeat me or develop me, depending on how I respond. So every cloud has a silver lining, and every problem comes with good news attached to it.

CHAPTER 25

WHAT KIND OF ANSWER DO YOU NEED?

I, even I, am he who comforts you.

—Isaiah 51:12

"Why, God?" is by far the most commonly asked God Question. A young couple asked that question on the day they received the news that their two-month-old daughter Marcia had a congenital disease that would cause her tremendous suffering and shorten her life.

Marcia wasn't digesting her food well nor growing as fast as she should. During a routine checkup, her mother asked if something might be wrong. After doing some tests, the doctor answered, "Marcia has cystic fibrosis."

The cystic fibrosis gene is recessive, so both parents must be carriers to pass it on. Neither of Marcia's parents knew of anyone who had ever had the disease. Yet here it was.

Marcia was my (Hal's) sister.

Growing up, there was never a morning my sister didn't have to take a pill to help her digest her food. By the time she was eight years old, she spent two hours every evening on a slant board with my mother patting on her back to loosen the phlegm in her lungs.

By age ten, Marcia started spending two weeks every year in the hospital fighting pneumonia. By age twelve, she was sleeping in an oxygen tent at night. At sixteen, Dad moved out. I later learned that divorce is common among parents of children with cystic fibrosis. The strain, pressure, and financial drain are more than most marriages can endure. The saddest memory of my young life came the night Marcia died. The doctor operated to remove mucus from her lungs. She never made it out of surgery. I can still hear my mother's sobs in her bedroom next to mine. Only one question was on our minds that night: "Why, God? Why?"

"God weeps with us so that we may one day laugh with Him." Jurgen Moltmann

---

Two Kinds of Answers

I know my mother's pain. I watched it up close. My father was more private about his suffering. Although he was raised in a religious home, his little girl's suffering raised questions beyond what his intellect could bear. For decades he questioned how God could be all-knowing, all-powerful, and all-loving and let his little girl experience such a thing.

When it comes to the question of suffering, there are two kinds of answers. One kind helps us mentally—these are logic-based answers. A second kind helps us emotionally—these are feeling-based answers. Most people in pain have a hard time listening to logic. What they need first is something that touches their hearts.

During the week I was writing this, a young man named Steve shared his story with our church. He arrived home one day to find the house empty, with a message that he was to join the family at the hospital. Upon entering the emergency room, he was greeted by the news that his father and brother had died in a traffic accident. A younger brother survived but lost a third of his brain. In the fourteen years since that accident, his brother had endured twenty surgeries.

Steve loves God. But understandably, he has struggled with trusting God after the losses he's experienced. In a moment of desperation, he even considered taking his own life. His pain was and continues to be very real. Fortunately, so is his faith. What has given Steve the resolve to continue to trust God? Two things: *compassion* and *community*.

During the dark night of his soul, members of his family and church wrapped their arms around him. There's a Yiddish proverb that says, "God gives burdens, also shoulders." Steve's community lent him shoulders to cry on and provided meals for the remaining family members, along with counsel, encouragement, and prayers. Steve received answers to his heart's questions that were served up with love. The answers touched his heart as well as his head.

When we hurt, it can be hard to believe in a God who cares. Knowing about free will may be intellectually encouraging, but it isn't emotionally satisfying. Personally, when I hurt, I want to be touched not just taught, comforted not just counseled.

Jesus gave us the ultimate answer to the problem of pain: He endured it Himself. When Steve asked the question, "How could God put anyone through this much pain?" God's answer was, "This pain was not of My doing, but I know how it feels. I suffered a significant level of pain, for you." In the midst of Steve's pain, he was touched by God's love—the deep love of a Father who not only says, "I'm sorry," but also says, "I know exactly how you feel."

It helps to know about free will. But it heals to know that God is present, especially when that knowledge is accompanied by the love of God's people.

Two Answers in One

I can't speak much about Steve's personal pain, but I can speak about my own. With the perspective of years, I can see that there were hints of God's compassion all over my sister's life and death. Marcia was endowed with exceptional gifts. Everyone who knew her loved her. The memories I carry of her are sweet and good.

Sometimes I wonder if the shortened span of her life might have been a gift from God. The Bible promises a wonderful afterlife for those who have trusted in Him. God's words play in my mind: *"No human mind has conceived . . . the things God has prepared for those who love him"* (1 Corinthians 2:9). Rather than suffer in her handicapped body for these last five decades, my sister has been experiencing wonders I cannot yet comprehend. I can believe in a God who rescues the hurting from their hurts. This hope helps both my head *and* my heart. I hope it will help yours too.

CHAPTER 26

WHICH ACT ARE WE LIVING IN?

Never again will there be in it an infant who lives but a few days, or an old man who does not live out his years.

—Isaiah 65:20

We live in a moment in time. Because it's *our moment*, it feels like things will always be the way they are right now. But judging God and history based on our limited experience is shortsighted. Have you ever walked in on the middle of a movie? Suppose the television is on while you're walking through the living room. The scene on the screen is really engaging, so you stand there and watch for a few minutes. Inevitably, a dozen questions race through your mind: *Why did the hero do that? How did they get there? Who's this person over here?* Without a context, much of what you're watching makes no sense.

Right now, planet Earth is in the middle scene of a three-act play. In Act I, a perfect world is created and then corrupted. In Act II, that corruption is played out while getting repaired. In Act III, the corruption is cleaned up and perfection restored. Judging the play by a brief glimpse of Act II is unreasonable. According to the Bible, which holds the script for the play, evil and suffering are only temporary. A day is coming when suffering will be wiped away and evil will be no more. The Bible says, *"He has set a day for judging the world with justice"* (Acts 17:31, NLT).

Why Let Suffering Continue?

Soon after the first Gulf War, a man named Richard came to my (Hal's) office. He said, "I want to know why God doesn't just wipe out Saddam Hussein and people like him in order to make the world a better place. People are dying! People are starving to death because of men like him! Why doesn't God just take those guys out?"

I knew some things about Richard. He had some struggles in his life, and he'd hurt some people along the way. He was concerned about the plight of the poor, yet he had never done anything to personally help with the poor. I read him 2 Peter 3:9: *"The Lord is not slow in keeping his promise, as some understand slowness. Instead he is patient with you, not wanting anyone to perish, but everyone to come to repentance."*

After a quick prayer, I decided to give Richard a straight dose of truth. "God doesn't 'take out' people like that because of you," I said. "If God chose to intervene in history like that, you'd be 'taken out' too."

He asked, "What do you mean?"

"He will wipe every tear from their eyes. There will be no more death or mourning or crying or pain, for the old order of things has passed away." Revelation 21:4

I replied, "Richard, God hasn't dealt with the evil in this world yet because He wants to extend grace *to you*. God is delaying in His cleaning up of evil, in part, because He wants to give you a chance to have your sin forgiven rather than judged. He is far more troubled by the pain inflicted on people than you are. But He loves you so much that He's been holding off on bringing judgment. To be fair to all, on that day, He'll have to judge you, and He'll have to judge me. And He doesn't want to judge you; He wants to give you grace instead." I then explained to Richard that grace was only a prayer away, that Christ paid for all the wrongs that he (Richard) and I had committed, and that all we had to do to receive His grace was believe in Him and accept His payment and forgiveness on our behalf.

The Full Story

The story of the world is the story of God and His perfect creation. He allowed for the possibility of evil and suffering by granting freedom of choice to His children. We chose to experience the evil and suffering (Act I). God then chose to make provision for our wrong choices by sending His Son to pay the penalty for them (Act II). This payment is available to all who will admit their need for it and trust Christ.

Because of the destructive power of evil, God will one day say, "Enough!" and judge the world, separating sin, evil, and death from all that is good and from those who have been forgiven of their evil by trusting in Christ (Act III). Paradise will then be fully restored in what the Bible calls *"a new heaven and a new earth"* (Revelation 21:1) in a world *"where righteousness dwells"* (2 Peter 3:13).

The Best Part

The best part of the story is that all the pain and suffering of this world will seem insignificant compared to the pleasure we experience in heaven. Most of us have had our share of bumps and bruises in this life. Compare yours to those of the Apostle Paul:

> *I have worked harder, been put in prison more often, been whipped times without number, and faced death again and again. Five different times the Jewish leaders gave me*

thirty-nine lashes. Three times I was beaten with rods. Once I was stoned. Three times I was shipwrecked. Once I spent a whole night and a day adrift at sea. I have traveled on many long journeys. I have faced danger from rivers and from robbers. I have faced danger from my own people, the Jews, as well as from the Gentiles. I have faced danger in the cities, in the deserts, and on the seas. . . . I have worked hard and long, enduring many sleepless nights. I have been hungry and thirsty and have often gone without food. I have shivered in the cold, without enough clothing to keep me warm. (2 Corinthians 11:23–27, NLT)

Yet, in the same letter, when Paul thought about what he would experience in the life to come, he said, *"Our present troubles are small and won't last very long. Yet they produce for us a glory that vastly outweighs them and will last forever!"* (2 Corinthians 4:17, NLT).

Suppose that on the first day of this year, you had a terrible day. You woke up with a migraine headache. At first, the pain was so bad that you were afraid you were going to die. Then it got so bad, you *wanted* to die. On the way to the doctor's office, you were hit by an uninsured motorist, totaling your car. The car was a Christmas present, and it was the car you'd always dreamed of owning. After leaving the doctor's and arriving at work, you found out that your company was downsizing, and your name was at the top of the list. The whole day went like that—terrible.

Then the next day, you woke up to a phone call from a competitor offering you a better job with twice the pay. Suppose the entire rest of the year turns out like this. You inherit $1 million from an unknown relative. You buy a lottery ticket with the first dollar, and you win another $10 million! Your children earn straight As; they are so good, their teachers ask to take you to dinner because they want to meet the parent of such outstanding children. Your marriage is perfect. You get voted "Person of the Year" by the local newspaper. You play golf with Jordan Spieth—and you win!

On December 31, someone asks you, "So, how was your year?" You answer, "It was unbelievable! Oh, yeah, that first day was a little rough, but everything else has gone so well, I had almost forgotten about it."

That's what it will be like in heaven.[112] That's Act III.

CHAPTER 27

CAN A LOVING GOD REALLY SEND PEOPLE TO HELL?

As the weeds are pulled up and burned in the fire, so it will be at the end of the age. The Son of Man will send out his angels, and they will weed out of his kingdom everything that causes sin and all who do evil.

—Matthew 13:40–41

The Bible teaches that hell is a real place and real people go there. That sounds heartless, doesn't it? How could a loving God send anyone to hell? Could you imagine sentencing one of your children to eternal misery?

Why God Had to Create Hell

One of the most anguishing God Questions is "Why did God create hell in the first place?" Like the problem of pain, this question screams at us because we don't want there to be suffering in the afterlife any more than we want there to be suffering in this life. Something deeply embedded in our souls does not want those we love to experience pain.

When you ask the question "Why hell?" you must immediately remind yourself that God doesn't want there to be a hell any more than we do. God never *sends* anyone there. Everyone in hell chooses it for themselves. God is *"not wanting anyone to perish, but everyone to come to repentance"* (2 Peter 3:9). The Creator never wants His creation to suffer. He creates for purposes of joy, not sorrow.

The simplest truth of the universe is that God created human beings to live in community with Him. Sin sentences people to separation from God. Jesus's sacrifice on the cross provided the means to erase the sentence. The only people who go to hell are those who decide they don't want Jesus and His sacrifice to apply to them.

Hell is the absence of God. In order to allow us the freedom of our choices, God had to allow for us to choose to say, "I want nothing to do with You. Go away and leave me alone." Everyone in hell will be very much alone.

For Justice's Sake

God *had* to create hell, or He would not be just or loving. All groups and governments develop systems of justice because human beings have an innate sense that evil cannot go unpunished. No one wants to live in a universe where the "Hitlers" get the same treatment as the "Mother Teresas." Evil must be paid for in order for there to be justice in the world. So God created hell, a place of eternal condemnation and destruction. It's the place where sin is paid for.

I don't believe that God *wanted* to create hell. His justice demands it. He cannot remain who He is—a just, moral being—without making provision for the payment of sin. So having created hell, God did everything He could to prevent any of His children from going there. He spared no expense, giving the life of His innocent Son to pay for the sins of the world. And He invites everyone to have their sins paid for by Christ's death.

If God is going to allow each of His children to have true free will, He cannot force His forgiveness on any of us. He must allow us to choose for ourselves. God says, "Choose. Sin must be paid for in order for there to be justice. You can pay the price yourself, or I will pay it for you." Without hell, humans would have no true choice because there would be no real and final consequences for our actions. When a mother says to her son, "If you touch one more cookie before you finish your dinner, I'll have to send you to your room," and the boy stuffs another cookie in his mouth, what's the one thing Mom must do? Send him to his room. Otherwise she loses her trustworthiness, respectability, and authority. The same is true with God; He must enforce the moral rules of the universe, or He Himself would be immoral.

"It is a problem which no theist will avoid and no honest thinker will try to avoid." Elton Trueblood

---

Because of Love

Imagine living in a world where fire is supposed to burn us, but it never does. Every time we reach our hand toward a flame, the flame goes out. Imagine living in a world where you couldn't experience any thrills because every time you strapped on a pair of skis or paddled out to a giant wave or jumped out of an airplane, the laws of nature were suspended. Imagine living in a world where every time you got mad at someone, it became physically impossible to express your anger. Psychologists have designed such a place; it's called a "padded cell."

God knew we couldn't be truly free if He created only a padded-cell world. So He created a world in which His children could explore, experience, make choices, and have their actions count. God loves His children so much that He wants them to be able to choose to love Him or not. So when the first humans sinned, God made provision for justice by the sacrifice of His Son. He said, "Come to Me." Though the gap between us and God was huge, God bridged it. He came all the way to our planet, and then into our hearts, whispering, "I love you, child. Come to Me."

Suppose some of His children refuse His invitation. Suppose they shake their bony fists at God and say, "I don't want to be forgiven! I don't want to have a relationship with You! I want nothing to do with You!" For God to continue to love, He must give these children the consequences of their choice. He must give them a place that is absent from His presence.

Summary

In effect, God is saying, "I did not create evil, but I allowed for it so that you could have the freedom to choose between right and wrong and the freedom to love Me. I don't like suffering, but I can make good come from it. Suffering won't always be part of the world. But for now, when you are in pain, know that I will be with you. I will hold your hand. I will walk with you in sorrow if you will let Me. Someday I will wipe it away once and for all. Someday your bliss will be so strong that your present suffering won't be worth comparing to it."

CHAPTER 28

IS THERE PURPOSE TO MY PAIN?

Consider it pure joy, my brothers and sisters, whenever you face trials of many kinds, because you know that the testing of your faith produces perseverance. Let perseverance finish its work so that you may be mature and complete, not lacking anything.

—James 1:2-4

It was a snowy winter evening, and I (Dan) was driving up the north side of the 11,500-foot Mount San Gorgonio in Southern California. I had the destination set in my GPS, but 30 minutes into the trip, I lost my signal and could only drive blindly toward my destination.

After two hours of futile wandering and failed attempts to find my campsite, I pulled over to find someone and ask them for directions. Within a few minutes, I saw headlights piercing the curtain of falling snow, heading toward me.

Desperately flashing my headlights, I hailed the ranger who stopped, and shared my dilemma. I told him where I was going. He said, "You can't get there from here."

I've heard that phrase before, mostly as the punchline to various jokes. When applied to real life, it never made sense to me.

"Are you saying it's impossible to get there?" I asked.

"No," he said. "You just can't get there from here. You have to return to your starting point. All your driving around on this side of the mountain has not been helpful. You must get to the other side of the mountain!"

No one wants to hear a message like that. If you're like me, you hate to retrace your steps. I dread redoing a project. When I've made a mess of things, I resist making them right.

From time to time the Father sends me signals that it's time to stop moving forward and reflect on where I am headed. Pain in particular, and difficulties for sure will stop me in my tracks. They force me to evaluate my life and direction.

It can work like the ranger in my mountain journey. One purpose for pain is to redirect us. It's the single most important agent that the Father uses to keep me from continuing down the wrong path.

One day I was praying about a painful situation. As I was praying, the Holy Spirit prompted me in an almost-audible way. He brought this thought to me, "Dan, it is your tension that makes you pay attention to me." I've never heard a truer word.

Tension Gets Our Attention

In the movie Shadowlands, C.S. Lewis says, "God whispers in our pleasure but he shouts in our pain. It's His megaphone to rouse a deaf world." Your problems are not punishment; they are wake-up calls from a loving heavenly Father. He isn't mad at you. But He will do whatever it takes to bring you back into relationship with Him. God allows us to enter into tension so we will seek Him.

I am nearly deaf to the voice of God when things are going well. However, when times are tough, I fall to my knees. I wish it weren't that way. The Father has repeatedly used tension to get my attention. I'm not the only. God speaks to Job that way in the Bible in Job 38.

The Lord riddles Job with questions about a series of catastrophes that have captured Job's attention. He provides the following perspective.

> *Where were you when I laid the earth's foundation? Tell me, if you understand. Who marked off its dimensions? Surely you know! Who stretched a measuring line across it? On what were its footings set, or who laid its cornerstone* —Job 38:4-6

This approach continues on for forty-one verses! God makes it clear to Job that God alone is sovereign, and He has things under control even if Job can't see it.

Job is tenderly invited to pause and turn toward the Father with his overwhelming pain and difficulty. God did that with scores of others throughout Scripture as well.

God gave us the book of Psalms as a template for how to respond to Him, especially when life gets tough. It is a work full of ranting, raving, doubts, fears, resentments, and deep passions combined with thanksgiving, praise, and statements of faith. Every possible emotion is catalogued in the Psalms as an example of how comfortable God the Father is along-side of us expressing our pain and emotions. When you read the confessions of David and others, realize this is how God wants you to worship him. He wants you to hold back nothing of what you feel.

If You're In Pain

Have you just been going through the motions spiritually? You may be on the verge of a struggle that has the ability to stop you in your tracks. Don't be surprised if a dose of pain comes your way. The good news is the Father is waiting to wrap His arms around you and offer His guiding presence. Jesus expressed this tender side of how He understands our need for care and direction.

> *I have longed to gather your children to-gether, as a hen gathers her chicks under her wings...* —Matthew 23:37

Jesus repeatedly offers His presence and direction. If we insist on ignoring Him, He will seek to draw us to Himself. But there is an easier way to connect with the Father.

Start telling Him that you are receptive to His leading. If you are going through a difficult season and are uncertain where God is in your pain, know that His presence is a whisper away. Quietly pray this throughout your day: "Dear Father, You have my attention. I want to get to know You intimately. I believe that you're serious about finding me. I want to be found. I long to get to know You. Help me in this painful season. I yield to You my trust. I want to follow you."

Take that step. You won't be disappointed.

QUESTION #5
WHICH IS RIGHT: EVOLUTION OR CREATION?

CHAPTER 29

WHICH IS RIGHT: EVOLUTION OR CREATION?

Great are the works of the LORD;
they are pondered by all who
delight in them.

—Psalm 111:2

During my senior year of high school I (Hal) stumbled upon a book that made claims I'd never heard before. The local school system had taught me that the fossil record represented an inviolable case for evolution. The book I was reading claimed that most fossils could be accounted for in one cataclysmic event: the universal flood of Genesis 6–9 in the Bible. According to the author, the amount of sediment created in that one flood would be enough to capture and compress every creature caught in it. Since the flood was universal, every species would be involved, which could explain how so many fossils came to be. Fascinated by this idea, I approached my favorite science teacher.

"Do you know about this?" I asked.

"I've heard about it," he said.

"I think you should tell your geology class about it!" I replied.

His response was, "I think *you* should tell my geology class about it."

So I did.

I was given the entire class period for my presentation of the effects of the Genesis flood. I entered the class with a few notes and a naive belief that I was doing everyone a favor—that my fellow classmates would want to know there was a viable alternative that explained the origin of the fossil record and offered a different view of the age of the earth.

Within five minutes the room was ablaze with a mixture of affirmation and ridicule. Everyone either loved or hated the idea; there was very little middle ground. A handful of students stayed afterward to thank me for confirming what they had already suspected, and another group hung around to question my intelligence. The son of a college professor fired a parting shot at me: "Well I'll be a monkey's uncle!" he spat as he sauntered out the door.

It was a baptism of fire for me. I knew the zeal and conviction with which many Christians approach their faith. It was the first time I had experienced the zeal and conviction of the scientific community.

I have since learned that one of the most hotly debated God Questions is the origin and development of our universe. "Which is right, evolution or creation?" isn't as personal as the question of pain and suffering, yet it's more fiercely contested than a World Cup trophy. Read the comments at the bottom of any blog defending either side of the issue, and you'll wonder if the author was questioning the commenter's mother's honor or sister's virtue. The question of evolution versus creation is more volatile than a uranium isotope.

If you've read anything on this subject, you know that Charles Darwin published a book in 1859 titled *On the Origin of Species* that stirred up this pot. What you might not know is that the pot had been boiling long before Darwin. People have debated the origins of the universe since just about the time someone pointed out that there *is* a universe.

In 1925, the whole issue reached fever pitch in a trial in Dayton, Tennessee, known as the Scopes Monkey Trial. Tennessee's legislature had passed a law prohibiting the teaching of evolution in schools. Opponents of the law found a former substitute teacher named John Thomas Scopes, who wasn't exactly sure he had ever actually taught evolution or not, to be the defendant.[113]

The trial took on national significance when famous attorneys stepped in on both sides of the case. The prosecution was led by William Jennings Bryan, a three-time Democratic presidential candidate and former secretary of state. The defense was represented by Clarence Darrow, a famous agnostic and criminal lawyer. During the proceedings, Darrow convinced Bryan to take the stand as an expert witness on the Bible. Though the trial ended in Scopes' conviction, Bryan was humiliated under cross-examination. Spencer Tracy starred in a movie based on Scopes' trial called *Inherit the Wind*.

The Debate

At issue in this great debate is whether or not the creatures we find on earth were *created* or *evolved* into what they are today. At deeper issue is whether the universe we live in came into existence on its own or if it had help from a higher power. Over the past hundred years or so, four major approaches have developed to answer the question of origins.

Natural Selection

The approach you've probably heard the most about is Darwin's. Darwin believed that pretty much all of nature could be explained by *natural selection*. That is, over time random mutations present some fortunate creatures with environmental advantages over their peers.

For instance, superior eyesight might allow one rodent to survive longer than another, enabling him to mate more often and create more rodents in his image, thus improving the species and presenting future rodent generations with more favorable circumstances. Being accidentally born with the ability to run, fly, or swim when your siblings cannot would produce the same results. Darwin postulated much smaller changes than these, but you get the point. Every once in a while, a minor mutation could produce a major advantage.

When a random chance mutation creates a superior version of any type of plant or animal, this superior specimen is usually able to produce more offspring than its contemporaries, passing forward its advanced survival mechanism to successive generations until finally those with lesser genes die off and those with the greater traits make up the entire species.

The advantage of this approach is that, at first glance, it's a simple and elegant explanation for all life on earth. It's also incredibly optimistic. Within our natural genes, it is possible to generate a never-ending succession of improvements within every species, including human beings. To a certain point of view, the greatest advantage of this option is that it requires no form of outside help. Belief in natural selection requires no belief in God. One could argue that this is a—if not *the*—major reason atheists and agnostics prefer this position almost exclusively.

Darwin predicted that those who came after him would discover links between species and explanations for the rise of complex systems, like the compound eye. Some say these things have happened. Others dispute this vehemently.

One virtual requirement of this way of thinking is a belief that the universe has to have been around forever or else managed to create itself. Since natural selection eliminates God from the equation, everything has to be accounted for by means of time and random chance.

Theistic Evolution

Theistic evolutionists attempt to harmonize their understanding of nature with an understanding of God. According to Francis Collins, the father of the Human Genome Project, this is "the dominant position of serious biologists who are also serious believers. . . . It is the view espoused by many Hindus, Muslims, Jews, and Christians."[114]

Theistic evolutionists believe that the universe was created *ex nihilo* ("out of nothing") around 13.73 billion years ago. They believe the universe bears an "anthropic principle"—that its details seem to have been carefully tended to support life as we know it. Like their naturalistic brethren, theistic evolutionists believe that natural selection is responsible for the biological complexity and diversity we see around us. For the most part, this branch of evolutionists thinks that once evolution got its start, it needed no further help to bring the universe to its current form. The group believes humans share a common ancestry with apes, but we are unique and distinct because of our spiritual nature.

Intelligent Design

A third option is intelligent design ("ID" for short). Frankly, I'm not completely sure what to make of this group. As a whole, they believe that our world is too full of irreducibly complex systems, anthropic coincidences, pure beauty, and grand design to have come to where it is without significant outside help. A few in this camp have suggested that life on earth came from the stars, that an alien race somehow "seeded" our world with the blueprints for life in order to get it started. This creative solution enables anti-supernatural IDers to maintain a vacuum of religious belief while affirming the obvious design behind our world.

Still, the vast majority of this group seem to be theists who have realized that there are legal constraints within the

American system of jurisprudence that make it expedient for them to omit "God" from the argument and settle for being able to say that some superior outside force or being must have started us off, and perhaps given us a push or two along the way.

In my opinion, at least, this group has done undeniably impressive work in the areas of biochemistry, genetics, and mathematics to show that the probability of higher life-forms developing by chance is virtually nil. Read some of their works, though, and then read their critics, and you'll get a sampling of the heat I felt way back in high school when I tried to introduce the idea of God to my geology class.

Considering that this position was born in 1991[115] and is therefore only getting started, I predict more impressive work in more fields of science to provide support for the concept of an intelligent designer responsible for the creation of life.

Biblical Creationism

Biblical creationists believe that discoveries in the natural world can shed light on the meaning of the words of the Bible, but whatever the Bible truly means is our final basis for truth. If natural evolution relies solely on scientific interpretation, biblical creationism starts with biblical interpretation. So, when Genesis 1 indicates that God created the world in six days, biblical creationists believe He did just that.

In the spirit of transparency, I will disclose that I put myself in this camp. In the sense that I believe there was (and is) an Intelligent Designer behind the creation and sustenance of our cosmos, you could say I believe in intelligent design. And in the sense that I am a theist who believes in microevolution,[116] you could say that I believe in theistic evolution. But because of the evidence presented in chapters 7–12 of this book, I believe the Bible is God's inerrant and infallible word to humanity. If something in nature doesn't seem to line up with something in Scripture, either we have misunderstood the meaning of the words of Scripture or further research and understanding of nature will eventually lead science to affirm the truth communicated by God in Scripture.

One great illustration of this is the Big Bang theory. For centuries, scientists believed that our universe had no beginning. Then, Einstein's theory of relativity, Hubble's research into the movement of the galaxies, and a few other seminal findings convinced almost everyone to espouse the Big Bang. The Bible describes the Big Bang in its opening phrase: *"In the beginning God created the heavens and the earth"* (Genesis 1:1). The Bible has taught that Creation had a big beginning since Moses penned its first words millennia ago. It just took science a while to catch up.

Biblical creationists believe that Genesis 1 and 2 accurately describe how the cosmos and life on planet Earth came into being. Some biblical creationists interpret these first two chapters to describe six literal twenty-four-hour days. Others believe the Hebrew word for "day" (*yom*) in this section of Scripture refers to long durations of time. The first group are usually called "Young Earth Creationists" because their interpretation leads to a belief that the earth is under ten thousand years old. The second group are called "Old Earth Creationists" because their interpretation leads to a belief that Earth could be as old as secular scientists believe it to be.

If the initial writing of Genesis had been done in modern English, Moses would have had many time-related words to choose from in his account of Creation. English has somewhere between 250,000 and 750,000 words at its disposal. Ancient Hebrew, however, had only about 8,000. In English, we have choices. When we want to express a brief period of time, we can use the words *moment, instant, jiffy,* or *tick.* If we want to express a long period of time, we have *era, eon, epoch, age,* or *period*. Hebrew is limited. The word *yom* carries the meaning of a portion of the daylight hours, all of the daylight hours, a twenty-four-hour period, or a long but finite period. For Moses, the only word available to express a long but finite period of time was *yom*.[117] Young Earth Creationists believe the Genesis account describes a twenty-four-hour day *yom*; Old Earth Creationists think *yom* is referring to a long period of time.

"I do not feel obligated to believe that the same God who has endowed us with sense, reason, and intellect has intended us to forgo their use." Galileo Galilei

---

Who holds the correct view? That's the big debate. As you dig into this topic, please beware of three things. One is your own natural bias, based on what you *want* to believe. Try to weigh the evidence based on truth rather than loyalty to friends who might fall into a certain camp. The second "beware" is of the passion you will find when you research this topic on your own. Try not to let someone's harsh words shock you. Many people feel they have a lot at stake on this particular God Question. Don't confuse name-calling for truth. The third "beware" is that this question may not be fully answered in this life. The question is important in so far as God's reputation is concerned, but if we can agree that there is a God who created, *how* He created may not be as important as some other questions, like *why* He created, the inspiration of Scripture, the deity of Christ, and how one gets to heaven.

It's Good to Ponder

In Psalm 111, the writer was contemplating how great God is. When he thought about all that God had created, he said, *"Great are the works of the LORD; they are pondered by all who delight in them*" (Psalm 111:2). Some scientists who appreciate the wonders of God found this verse so helpful, they embossed it on the door to their laboratory. If you visit the prestigious Cavendish Laboratory at Cambridge University, you'll find Psalm 111:2 imprinted on the oak entrance door.

Cavendish's founder, James Maxwell, developed the theory of electromagnetism as he pondered the works of the Lord. I hope you'll take some delight in pondering the creation of our cosmos over the next few chapters. Such pondering can lead to good things!

CHAPTER 30

DID OUR UNIVERSE HAVE A BEGINNING?

*In the beginning
God created the heavens
and the earth.*

—Genesis 1:1

Has the universe always existed? Or did it have a beginning? Many people think the evolution versus creation questions started when Darwin published his *On the Origin of Species* in 1859. But the argument actually goes back far further. For thousands of years, sides have been drawn about the origins of our cosmos.

A Little History

On one side of the debate are the Hindus, who believe that the universe is eternal, going through repeating cycles of creation, destruction, and rebirth, with each cycle lasting approximately 4.32 billion years. On the other side of the debate are the Jews, who believe that the universe is finite, having its beginning *"in the beginning"* (Genesis 1:1).

The ancient Greeks fell into the infinite universe camp, believing the universe was unchanged and static. The Greeks thought of science as a branch of philosophy. Rather than measure and verify, they used logic to put together principles of nature. Considering that Pythagoras reasoned the earth was a sphere, Aristarchus deduced the distance to the sun, and Eratosthenes estimated the circumference of the earth, they were surprisingly good at it!

When Christianity was born, its proponents adopted the Jewish Scriptures, contending for a finite universe. As Islam arose, its philosophers joined the argument on the side of a finite beginning as well. Yet even within one religious system, the debate was never settled. In his *Principia*, Sir Isaac Newton, a committed Christian, described a static steady-state universe that was infinite in size and duration. Albert Einstein initially built upon this model, advocating for an infinite steady-state universe.

Is the Universe Finite or Infinite?

Ironically, the first nail to penetrate the coffin of an infinite universe was Einstein's General Theory of Relativity. In 1915, Einstein proved the direct relationship between space and time. Because of the nature of space-time, the theory of general relativity requires that the universe be constantly expanding. Anything expanding is not yet infinite, which means that the universe is finite. The universe cannot have existed since infinity past or it would be infinite in size. It must have had a beginning.

At first, Einstein was irritated at the idea of a finite universe. He realized that if the universe is expanding away from a point, it had to have a beginning at that point, and if the universe had a beginning, then it had to have a "Beginner." Einstein so disliked this idea that for several years he included what he called a "cosmological constant" in his formulas in order to make the effect of an expanding universe appear to go away. But in 1929, Edwin Hubble published findings that the nearby galaxies are moving away from our Milky Way galaxy at a speed directly proportionate to their distance from us. Upon studying Hubble's findings, Einstein conceded that the universe is indeed expanding, disavowed his "cosmological constant," and admitted that including it in his General Theory of Relativity was the greatest mistake of his career. For his research, Hubble was awarded the Gold Medal of the Royal Astronomical Society in 1940.

The Big Bang

What kind of a beginning did our universe have? Cosmologists believe that all the matter in the universe came from one infinitely dense, hot ball. In 1949, Fred Hoyle described this hot beginning on a BBC radio program as "the Big Bang." The phrase caught on. Some think Hoyle meant the term derogatively. Scientists, like the rest of us, don't like it when their beliefs conflict with the evidence. Hoyle and the majority of scientists at the time believed in the Steady State theory. But evidence continued to mount that our universe had its beginning in one great expansion from zero space to massive space in an instant.

In 1968, Steven Hawking, George Ellis, and Roger Penrose published documents that added measurements of time and space to Einstein's General Theory.[118] These papers concluded that prior to the moment of the Big Bang, time and space did not exist!

I'm fond of Bill Bryson's description of this remarkable event. Bryson asks us to imagine packing every ounce of matter in the universe into a space the size of a proton, then shrinking it so much further that the space actually occupies no space at all. This one bit of future-universe is called a "singularity." Bryson said,

> It is natural but wrong to visualize the singularity as a kind of pregnant dot hanging in a dark, boundless void. But there is no space, no darkness. The singularity has no "around" around it. There is no space for it to occupy, no place for it to be. We can't even ask how long it has been

*there—whether it has just lately popped into be-
ing, like a good idea, or whether it has been there
forever, quietly awaiting the right moment. Time
doesn't exist. There is no past for it to emerge
from.*

And so, from nothing, our universe begins.

*In a single blinding pulse, a moment of glo-
ry much too swift and expansive for any form of
words, the singularity assumes heavenly dimensions, space beyond conception. In the first lively second . . . is produced gravity and the other
forces that govern physics. In less than a minute
the universe is a million billion miles across and
growing fast. There is a lot of heat now, ten billion degrees of it, enough to begin the nuclear
reactions that create the lighter elements—prin-
cipally hydrogen and helium, with a dash . . . of
lithium. In three minutes, 98 percent of all the
matter there is or will ever be has been produced.
We have a universe. It is a place of the most won-
drous and gratifying possibility, and beautiful,
too. And it was all done in about the time it takes
to make a sandwich.*[119]

Since Hubble's discovery, evidence for the Big Bang has poured
in from multiple sources. Decisive proof of our finite beginning
came from an unexpected quarter. Two Bell Laboratory scientists
named Arno Penzias and Robert Wilson spent a year trying to
quiet the background noise they were hearing from the huge Bell
antenna set up in Holmdel, New Jersey. The two tried everything
they could think of to create a clear signal. In desperation, they
phoned Princeton University to see if the researchers there might
be able to help them diagnose their problem.

In a twist of fate, the lead researcher, Robert Dicke, had been working to find a phenomenon called "cosmic background radiation." Twenty years earlier, a Russian scientist named George Gamow had predicted that if we were able to listen far enough into space (about 90 billion trillion miles), we should be able to hear the "cosmic background radiation" left over from the Big Bang.

Gamow hypothesized that if the universe had been forged in a massive cosmic explosion, the first photons would be detectable as microwaves. The Russian even suggested that these microwaves could be picked up by the big Bell Labs antenna in Holmdel. Neither Penzias and Wilson nor the Princeton research team had read Gamow's paper. But Dr. Dicke knew immediately what the Bell Lab workers had found. "Well, boys, we've just been scooped," he remarked after he hung up the phone.[120] Penzias and Wilson received the Nobel Prize in 1978. Their discovery of cosmic microwave background radiation proved decisively that we live in a finite universe.

"Beginnings are always messy." John Galsworthy

If the Universe Is Finite

Knowing that the universe is finite doesn't resolve our question about evolution versus creation, but it does clarify things a bit. For one, it keeps the creationist viewpoint on the playing court because there was indeed a beginning.

The Hindu view of a universe vacillating through cycles of expanse and collapse is no longer an option. The Big Bang beginning posits a universe with a massive energy buildup that will eventually have a complete energy breakdown. The Second Law of Thermodynamics (also known as the Law of Entropy) indicates that the universe is winding down, like a clock. One day all energy will be finally converted to matter, and the heavens and the earth will die a cold, lifeless death. (Unless something or *Someone* intervenes.)

When Will the Universe End?

If you'd like to know the exact time of our demise, just tease out this little equation and you can calculate the date and time for yourself: Protons each consist of at least three quarks. Quarks decay into antiquarks, pions, positive electrons, and electromagnetic radiation at the rate of once per proton every 10^{32} years. Now all you have to do is multiply that very large number (10^{32}) times three . . . or more. First, you'll have to find out how many protons have more than three quarks. Then, you'll need to figure out the decay rate of antiquarks, pions, electrons, and radiation, along with what each of them decays into. And then . . .

You get the point. Unless God intervenes (and there's a distinct possibility that He will[121]), our universe will be around for a long, long time—though not an *infinite* length of time. For that, you'll have to get on board the New Earth, which we will talk about in chapters 33 and 34.

Big Bang's great beginning is the starting point for evolution's timed equation that *time plus chance equals everything in existence*. Scientists currently believe that the Big Bang took place around 13.73 billion years ago. If that's true, evolutionists must squeeze all the "plus chance" into less than fourteen billion years. Is that enough time for chance to create the world we live in?

Because there was a beginning to time and space, we live in a closed system. Time, in our universe, is limited. Space is limited too. The universe has a finite past and future and a finite (though expanding) space it fills. Yet we can imagine *eternity*, and we can imagine *infinite space*. We can also imagine a nonmaterial, or *spiritual*, world.

The Bible says that God has *"set eternity in the human heart"* (Ecclesiastes 3:11). These three images of infinite time, infinite space, and a spiritual realm may be part of the subtle whisper of eternity in our spirits, calling to us that there is something and Someone more that we were made for.

CHAPTER 31

IF GOD MADE THE UNIVERSE, WHO MADE GOD?

*Before the mountains were born
or you brought forth the whole world,
from everlasting to everlasting
you are God.*

—Psalm 90:2

Until roughly a hundred years ago, no one could say for sure if the matter in the universe was infinitely old or created in space and time. Anti-supernaturalists reasoned that if matter was eternal, it needed no creator. But if matter was created, there are only two options: (1) It was created by something outside space-time, or (2) it created itself. The second answer is, at best, absurd and, more logically, impossible, which leaves us with only one answer: *Our universe was created by a supernatural Creator.*

Modern science relies on the Law of Causality as the foundation for experimentation, verification, and discovery. In chapter 1 we said that every effect must have a cause. Everything that exists was *caused* by something. Causality plays a critical role in answering the question of Creation. Since the universe exists, it must have been caused. Who or what could cause everything? Theologians answer, "Only an Uncaused Causer could create from nothing." Thomas Aquinas called Him "The Unmoved Mover."

In order to create space-time, the Uncaused Causer must exist *outside* of space-time. For years this may have seemed like a convenient theological construct. After all, how could anything exist outside of space-time? The idea was purely theoretical. Then, a few decades ago, scientists started experimenting with nuclear particle accelerators to discover the makeup of things smaller than an atom.

Our Multidimensional Universe

Most of us were under the impression that there were four—and only four—dimensions to our universe: height, width, depth, and time. As scientists began smashing atoms, they discovered a mini-universe of subatomic particles. This gave them the opportunity to invent names for these newly discovered entities, and they have done so with gusto. The smaller the particle, the more exotic its name. Last chapter I mentioned *quarks* and *antiquarks*. We also know of things called *leptons, bosons, muons, gluons, hadrons, baryons, mesons, gravitinos,* and *wavicles*. Scientists around the world have built colossal machines to study the tiniest fragments. They've also given some clever names to their machines—like "the Tevatron," "the Betatron," "the Large Hadron Collider," and "the Relativistic Heavy Ion Collider."

"Since motion must be everlasting and must never fail, there must be some everlasting first mover, one or more than one." Aristotle

---

Once upon a time, we believed that every particle could be located within our four dimensions. But when all the smashing began, we suddenly found out that predicting and charting the exact location of a quark, for instance, was impossible. The science of quantum mechanics was born, which said that a given subatomic particle could be located in a *range* of possible locations. This new field of study showed us that small particles acted as much like waves as particles of matter. Sometimes these little rascals are in one place, sometimes in another, and sometimes they seem to leap from one place to another without actually moving through space. It took a while, but someone finally figured out that particles weren't *leaping* exactly. They were getting from point A to point B by traveling through a dimension outside of our space-time continuum. Think of it like a ball getting from one end of a room to another. Instead of rolling down the inside of the wall, the ball rolls through a door, down the hall, and back into the room by a second door at the other end of the room. That hallway is in another dimension.

This is getting to sound a bit like science fiction, but it's all true. Scientists now believe that there are more than four dimensions. Many more. The science of string theory postulates ten or eleven dimensions; one branch, called "superstring theory," hypothesizes twenty-six dimensions. It's mind-bending, I know. My brain feels warped trying to think about it. But stay with me a little longer.

The Bible pictures God as being outside of our time dimension: *"This grace was given us in Christ Jesus before the beginning of time"* (2 Timothy 1:9). The Bible also says, *"By faith we understand that the universe was formed at God's command, so that what is seen was not made out of what was visible"* (Hebrews 11:3).

Extra Dimensions and Jesus

Dr. Hugh Ross thinks these other dimensions may explain how Jesus was able to walk through walls after His resurrection. *"On the evening of that first day of the week, when the disciples were* together, with the doors locked for fear of the Jewish leaders, Jesus came and stood among them" (John 20:19).

Ross wrote,

> Jesus proved His physical reality by allowing the disciples to touch Him and by eating food in front of them. Though it is impossible for three-dimensional physical objects to pass through three-dimensional physical barriers without one or the other being damaged, Jesus would have no problem doing this in His extra dimensions. . . . He could simultaneously translate the first dimension of His physicality into the fourth dimension, the second into the fifth, and the third into the sixth. Then He could pass through the walls of the room and transfer His three-dimensional body from the fourth, fifth, and sixth dimensions back into the first, second, and third.[122]

Philippians 2:7 describes Jesus's transition from divinity to incarnate humanity as "*he made himself nothing by taking the very nature of a servant, being made in human likeness.*" The phrase "made himself nothing" is made up of two words in Greek (*ekenosen morphen*). The first is a verb that means literally "to make of no effect." The second is the word from which we get our word "morph" (as in "Mighty Morphin Power Rangers") or "metamorphosis." To morph means to change the form of. What if a portion of Jesus's temporary change of form included "making of no effect" some of His extra-dimensional capabilities? Perhaps He reassumed those dimensional abilities once He had accomplished His work on the cross. This would not only explain His ability to walk through walls but is an exciting forecast for those who one day hope to receive resurrected bodies as well!

The Apostle Paul described Christians' new bodies this way:

> So will it be with the resurrection of the dead. The body that is sown is perishable, it is raised imperishable; it is sown in dishonor, it is raised in glory; it is sown in weakness, it is raised in power; it is sown a natural body, it is raised a spiritual body. (1 Corinthians 15:42–44)

Imagine living someday in ten or eleven or twenty-six dimensions! That would certainly provide a new level of thrills, to say nothing of new possibilities for learning, discovery, and adventure!

What If Time Was Two-Dimensional?

While we're on the subject of other potential dimensions, let's think about the possibility that time might have more than one dimension. String theorists are still wrestling with extra space dimensions, but a few other scientists are exploring the possibility that time may have more dimensions as well.

Consider what we already know about time:

1. It had a beginning.

2. It only goes forward; it can't run in reverse.

3. It can't be stopped.

With our minds already stretched by thinking about so many spatial possibilities, these limits seem terribly confining, don't they? When you think about it, time as we know it is really half a dimension.[123] It's like a line running only in one direction. What if that line could actually run in two directions?

A line is a one-dimensional object. What if time were two-dimensional? Think of it like a piece of paper. In our space-time framework, we can only move forward in time. Someone who is able to navigate forward and backward, plus left and right, would be able to move in and out of our time line at will. He would also be able to see every moment of our time line, knowing our end from our beginning. Maybe this is part of what it means to be eternal.

Second Peter 3:8 says, *"But do not forget this one thing, dear friends: With the Lord a day is like a thousand years, and a thousand years are like a day."* Psalm 90:4 says, *"A thousand years in your sight are like a day that has just gone by, or like a watch in the night."*

Who Made God?

The short answer to the question "If God made the universe, who made God?" is, *no one.* God is the Uncaused Causer who created our world out of nothing.[124] He could do this because He is an all-powerful, all-knowing Creator who exists outside our limited dimensionalities.

The Bible describes God as many types of perfection: all-powerful, all-knowing, all-sufficient, all-loving, omnipresent, and much more. One of His less-glamorous perfections is His *eternality*. In Exodus 3:14 He revealed Himself to Moses as "I AM WHO I AM." The phrase in Hebrew is *Ehyeh-Asher-Ehyeh*. *Ehyeh* is the first-person singular imperfect form of the verb "to be" or "to exist." When Moses asked, "Who are you?" God responded by saying, "I am who I am," or "I am that I am." In fact, it's more profound than that. He was saying, "I *am* fully and always have been. I exist completely, everywhere, at all times. I am absolutely present in all moments, at all times." Human language has limits. I believe what the Lord was trying to communicate was His awesome eternality that occupies every space and every moment, in time, above time, beneath time, around time, at all times, at the same time. For such a Being, creating our universe would be mere recreational activity.

How did our world come into being? The simplest answer is "God made it." He created time and space where and when there was no time or space. Yes, it's mind-blowing—and also exceedingly encouraging. Not only because it's the simplest possible explanation for how our world came to be but also because of what it says about us humans and our place in this universe.

Psalm 139

Three thousand years ago, King David thought about God, the cosmos, his place in the cosmos, and his place in the heart of God. David recorded in his journal:

> You have searched me, LORD,
>> and you know me.
> You know when I sit and when I rise;
>> you perceive my thoughts from afar.
> You discern my going out and my lying down;
>> you are familiar with all my ways. (verses
>> 1–3)

David was thinking about God's omniscience and omnipresence. He continued,

> Before a word is on my tongue
>> you, LORD, know it completely.
> You hem me in behind and before,
>> and you lay your hand upon me. (verses
>> 4–5)

David was thinking about what theologians call God's "foreknowledge." God knew every word the king would say because of His eternality. He exists outside of what we know as "time."

> *Such knowledge is too wonderful for me,*
> *too lofty for me to attain.* (verse 6)

David's response is typical of a person who gets past all the questions *about* God and starts thinking *of* God. In his musing, David realized that because of all of God's perfections, he was known at a level he had always dreamed of. He realized that the limitless Creator of everything was intimately interested in him.

Going back to God's attributes, David asked,

> *Where can I go from your Spirit?*
> *Where can I flee from your presence?*
> *If I go up to the heavens, you are there;*
> *if I make my bed in the depths, you are*
> *there.*
> *If I rise on the wings of the dawn,*
> *if I settle on the far side of the sea,*
> *even there your hand will guide me,*
> *your right hand will hold me fast.* (verses
> 7–10)

The practical application of God's perfections is that there is nowhere David (or anyone) could go where God can't know him, hold him, and help him.

Faced with the worst possible scenario, David reasoned,

> *If I say, "Surely the darkness will hide me*
> *and the light become night around me,"*
> *even the darkness will not be dark to you;*
> *the night will shine like the day,*
> *for darkness is as light to you.* (verses
> 11–12)

David's conclusion about God's eternality was:

> *Search me, God, and know my heart;*

test me and know my anxious thoughts.
See if there is any offensive way in me,
*   and lead me in the way everlasting.* (verses
    23–24)

The king knew that God could see beyond height, width, depth, and time into the spiritual and mental dimensions of his heart. Such knowledge is too lofty for humans to attain but completely natural to God, who, after all, brought it all into being—and more.

CHAPTER 32

HOW DID IT ALL BEGIN?

You alone are the LORD.
You made the heavens, even the
highest heavens, and all their starry
host, the earth and all that is on it,
the seas and all that is in them.
You give life to everything.

—Nehemiah 9:6

Children love to hear their parents tell stories about "when you were born" and "when you were little," which makes me think that how we got here and where we came from is very important to us. God knows this. In the book of Genesis, He carefully documented our planet's beginnings, our species' beginnings, and the early stories of what formed and shaped human society. In some ways, the book of Genesis is humanity's family photo album. It doesn't cover every detail of our early days, but God filled it with pictures that fulfill our longing to know the highlights of our beginnings.

Psalm 12:6 claims, *"The words of the LORD are flawless, like silver purified in a crucible, like gold refined seven times."* Genesis 1 contains the beautiful and flawless words of how the universe began. We may not fully understand all the nuances of this first chapter of Scripture, but what we do understand sheds significant light on how our world began.

Genesis 1 is both a masterpiece of literature and a miracle of recorded history. From a literary standpoint, the Creation story is told with symmetry, style, and grace. The chronology begins with God doing work (see Genesis 1:1) and ends with Him resting from His work (see Genesis 2:3).

Verse 1 provides the introduction: *"In the beginning God created the heavens and the earth."* The four fundamental determinations of physics are time, space, matter, and causality. They're all present in this first verse. "In the beginning [time] God created [causality] the heavens [space] and the earth [matter]." Verse 2 supplies the problem: *"The earth was formless and empty."* The formlessness needs to be formed, and the emptiness needs to be filled. Verse 1 is a snapshot from outer space. Verse 2 begins a video narrative from the vantage point of planet Earth.

Symmetry

Days One through Three are about forming. Days Four through Six are about filling. Each day's creation has a filling three days later:

Days of Forming	Days of Filling
1 Light formed	4 Lights give light to the earth
2 Water formed in the sky	5 Birds fill the sky
2 Water formed on the surface	5 Creatures fill the sea
3 Dry land formed	6 Animals fill the land
3 Vegetation formed	6 Plants for food fill the land

There is a rhythm and majesty to the Creation account. At the beginning of each day comes the announcement, *"And God said, 'Let there be . . .'"* Five of the six days include an acknowledgement, *"And it was so."* The day's descriptions conclude with *"And God saw that it was good,"* followed by the benediction *"And there was evening, and there was morning— the _____ day."*

Science Confirms the Bible

Read through a few commentaries on Genesis 1 and you'll find that the more we learn about science, the clearer we understand God's description of Creation. Older commentaries tend to be sketchier on the details of how things actually happened. Newer commentaries tend to touch on deeper detail with greater accuracy. This seems a little backward, doesn't it? After all, if the Bible is flawless, shouldn't it be shedding light on science instead of science shedding light on it?

Not really. What is happening in the study of origins these days is similar to what has happened in many areas of science in modern history. Science is confirming and clarifying the Bible's truths.

"In the crucible of scientific investigation, the Bible has proven invariably to be correct. No other book, ancient or modern, can make this claim; but then, no other book has been written (through men) by God." Hugh Ross

---

For instance, once upon a time, Europeans believed the world was flat. The Bible describes the earth as a sphere—*"the circle of the earth"* (Isaiah 40:22). No one believed it until Columbus sailed across the Atlantic.

In AD 150, Ptolemy cataloged 1,022 stars. For centuries, people thought that was about the right number. Yet the Bible indicates there are billions (if not more).[125] Once telescopes were invented, scientists looked heavenward and confirmed the Bible's claims.

For much of history, people thought the universe was in a steady, eternal, and unchanging state. Isaiah 40:22 claims that God is *"stretch[ing] out the heavens."* In the 1920s, Edwin Hubble documented that the galaxies are moving away from each other in what we now know is an expanding universe.

Science doesn't always get it right. It builds on one insight after another. But when science does get it right, it always confirms the teachings of Scripture.

What Happened in the Beginning?

The Bible begins from the vantage point of outer space. Genesis 1:1 says, *"In the beginning God created the heavens and the earth."* Of course it starts there. In that first moment there was *only* outer space. Earth didn't exist until after the Big Bang. In one chaotic moment, God *"created."* The Hebrew word is *bara'*, meaning "created from nothing." The word will appear two more times in the Creation account. The rest of the time, the author uses *'asa*, which means "to form," "to fashion," or "to manufacture by labor." The verb *bara'* is only used of God because only God can create things out of nothing.

The vantage point shifts in Genesis 1:2: *"Now the earth was formless and empty, darkness was over the surface of the deep, and the Spirit of God was hovering over the waters."* The only witness to this creative activity was the Holy Spirit. He's watching and reporting now from just above the earth's surface. At this point, the earth is dark. Particles are coalescing. Debris is everywhere. As the initial mass that will become Earth gathers more and more debris to itself, it generates greater gravitational attraction. Scientists believe that during planetary formation, a planet's atmosphere moves from opaque to translucent to transparent over a vast amount of time. In this earliest report, the earth's atmosphere is still opaque. The dust surrounding the surface is so thick that no light gets through.

Right now, the earth is *"formless."* Chunks of space debris are impacting the surface like huge bombs. Gravity is bringing atoms together. A sphere is forming. The earth is *"empty."* Life requires photosynthesis. Because light can't penetrate to the surface yet, no life is possible.

Day One

Day One began with God's directive, *"Let there be light"* (verse 3). At His command, light appeared. Earth was clearing her atmosphere, moving from opaque to translucent. You wouldn't be able to see very far in these conditions, but light was becoming distinguishable from what was once only darkness.

How did this happen? Gravity would pull some debris earthward. The sun would pull more its direction. In theory, our world should have a thicker atmosphere than it does. Cosmologists tell us that the greater a planet's surface gravity and distance from its star, the heavier and thicker its atmosphere.[126] Earth breaks this rule, leading astronomers to believe that during this time a collision took place. Our home was hit by a mass roughly the size of Mars. This planet-sized object was absorbed into Earth's core, blasted most of our atmosphere into space, and the jetsam from the impact circled Earth and eventually formed into our moon.

This impact created benefits for us. It thinned our atmosphere enough to permit light to reach our surface. It added enough mass to Earth's gravity that we could hold onto water vapor, but not so much gravity that we would retain lighter, life-threatening gases in our atmosphere. It increased Earth's iron content enough to support abundant sea life, which in turn supports advanced land life. The crash seeded Earth's interior with radioisotopes. These isotopes gave off heat that warmed our core and created significant volcanic activity. That volcanic activity created elevation upheavals that eventually breached the waterline, creating dry land. The crash also gradually slowed Earth's rotation rate so that increasingly complex life-forms could be introduced. And it fixed the tilt of our axis, which enabled seasons and prevented extreme temperatures that could extinguish life.[127]

Day Two

On Day Two, God orchestrated *"a vault between the waters to separate water from water"* (verse 6). It was the beginning of the water cycle, one of the most important processes for giving life to our world. Water vapor forms into clouds in our atmosphere, descending as rain, snow, sleet, or hail to water the earth. Evaporation (primarily from our oceans) sends the water skyward to descend on land again.

Day Three

Day Three had two *"Let there bes."* The first was dry ground; the second was vegetation. Compared to other planets, Earth experiences a high level of tectonic activity. This allows it to maintain about 30 percent of its surface as dry ground. This 30/70 land/water surface split enables a high degree of biological diversity. The natural process of erosion continually washes dirt, rocks, and sand back into our oceans. Land continues to be renewed by new deposits through volcanoes and tectonic plate activity. Tides enrich our coastal zones and continental shelves with nutrients, simultaneously sanitizing them of waste and toxins. Without these processes, life would be threatened, and over time Earth would become a uniform ball of rock covered a mile and a half deep in water.

The second creative act that took place on Day Three was the production of plants. It's possible that the Hebrew words for these forms of plant life could include primitive species. At any rate, since plants-as-food-source takes place on Day Five, the purpose of these initial plants was probably to begin the process of oxygen production and land fertilization and preservation.

Day Four

Day Four's command was *"Let there be lights in the vault of the sky to separate the day from the night, and let them serve as signs to mark sacred times, and days and years, and let them be lights in the vault of the sky to give light on the earth*" (verses 14–15). Apparently, Earth's atmosphere has now gone from translucent to transparent. Most likely, factors such as air pressure and temperature, humidity, and a high planetary rotation rate kept a constant cloud cover over the earth. A slowing rotation rate, plant metabolism of carbon dioxide, and stabilizing air pressure and temperature made direct sight of the sun and moon possible. Editorially, Moses explained that the purpose of the two great lights was not to be worshiped as gods, as many contemporary cultures were doing, but to serve as servants of mankind.[128]

Day Five

Day Five opens with God's decree to

> "*Let the water teem with living creatures, and let birds fly above the earth across the vault of the sky.*" *So God created the great creatures of the sea and every living thing with which the water teems and that moves about in it, according to their kinds, and every winged bird according to its kind.* (verses 20–21)

This is the second time God had "created from nothing" (*bara'*). Since the Big Bang, God had been forming things out of the material He first created in verse 1.

Here He created three types of species that possess intellect, will, and emotions, or what the Hebrews call *nephesh*. Mammals and birds have the unique capacity to respond to humans. They exhibit happiness, fear, and sorrow. Some can be tamed by us, others relate to us, still others fear or threaten us. Every step in this Creation story leads us closer to an intimate conclusion: God is preparing a habitat for humans to live in and thrive. Everything done is done with us in mind!

Day Six

The final creating day came with a flurry. God said,

> *"Let the land produce living creatures according to their kinds: the livestock, the creatures that move along the ground, and the wild animals, each according to its kind." . . . God made the wild animals according to their kinds, the livestock according to their kinds, and all the creatures that move along the ground according to their kinds.* (verses 24–25)

What you can't miss is that God is putting an adaptive lock on His creatures. They can only breed *"according to their kinds."*

The Hebrew words for these animals are *behema*, *remes*, and *hayya*. They are all *nephesh*. *Behema* are mostly herbivores, many of which will be domesticated for food and labor. *Remes* is sometimes used for reptiles; here the word clearly refers to short-legged land mammals—rabbits, rodents, and other things that will provide food for us (and sometimes clean up food scraps after us). *Hayya* are mainly carnivores; some will be hunted for food, others will become pets.

The climax of the account comes in verse 26: *"Let us make mankind in our image."* Verse 27 gives the third and final use of *bara'*: *"So God created mankind in his own image."* Humans are something completely new. Only humans are created in the image of God. Only humans possess something that stamps us as "like God" in morals, aspirations, self-awareness, creativity, and capacity to reason on a high level.

The story concludes with God blessing His image-bearers, commissioning them to *"Be fruitful and increase in number; fill the earth and subdue it"* (verse 28). In verse 29 He gives us rulership over every living creature and grants us the right to eat anything we please. He then awards Himself His highest grade: *"God saw all that he had made, and it was very good"* (verse 31).

Day Seven

The postscript to Creation is a principle unto itself. God completed His creative activity by resting, as a lifestyle example to us (Genesis 2:1–3).[129]

This is our story. Or at least its beginning. With all His creativity—and the greatest of care—God joyfully fashioned a racetrack for the human race. This is our home movie, carefully preserved, with high-density detail of the highlights. From this account it is easy to see that we are unfathomably loved by an infinite God, for we were greatly prepared for by His supernatural acts of *bara'* and *'asa*.

CHAPTER 33

HOW CAN YOU *NOT* BELIEVE IN EVOLUTION?

*"Present your case," says the L*ORD*.
"Set forth your arguments,"
says Jacob's King.*
—Isaiah 41:21

The theory of evolution is so ingrained in our Western school systems that it's hard *not* to believe it. In some ways evolutionists are like sports fans. They cheer their victories and dispute every defeat. I (Hal) had a chance to experience this up close one evening several years ago.

My children were educated in the Vista public school system. Vista is a quiet little city at the north end of San Diego County. Nothing much happens here. But in the early 1990s our school district found itself with a majority of Christians seated on its school board. One day a curious citizen asked if the board would ever consider including Intelligent Design in the science curricula as an alternative to evolutionary theory. The inquiry was made in some sort of official way that required it to be included in the school board's next meeting agenda.

When the agenda was published, this unsuspecting group of elected representatives had to move their normally quiet meeting to one of the district's gymnasiums to accommodate the crowd. I must have been feeling bored that night because I suggested to my wife that we attend and see how our little city handled such things.

We arrived to a media circus. Camera crews were everywhere. Protesters had driven for miles to block the initiative. People had made placards. Several were chanting slogans. District protocol required anyone who wished to address the board be given two minutes to speak their piece. The line for speech-making stretched out the door. As the meeting started, the chairman reassured us all that the board had no intention of changing the school's science curriculum. I thought that would calm the crowd. It didn't. Placards continued to wave, and the chanting volume increased.

Lori and I watched the frenzy for about an hour before heading home. I've been to hockey games before. These fans were more loyal and demonstrative! The only thing that could have made the evening more thrilling would have been somebody selling popcorn.

Darwinists have reasons for what they believe. These are presented in school classrooms every week. For the sake of balance, I'll devote this chapter to evolution's shortcomings so you can make an informed decision about how our world became what it is today.

Darwinian Downsides
Statistics point away from evolution.
At its core, evolution is about reproduction. The fittest of each species produce more offspring. This directs the development of each subsequent generation. Reproduction is far more complicated than Darwin imagined. On a micro level, it's made up of reactions from amino acids, proteins, and enzymes. The superstars of our reproductive system are DNA and RNA. These

little wonders carry and decipher the information necessary to reproduce cells and creatures. Between all these (and more), there is enough information capacity in a single human cell to store more than three times the amount of information in all thirty volumes of the *Encyclopedia Britannica*.[130] The complexity of anatomy is mind-boggling! It defies simple explanations and chance progress or improvements.

In order to have natural selection, you must have a reproductive process. How could such a process develop by chance? (Follow this for a minute. The math might get a little tedious, but you'll get the point.) A single cell needs a minimum of 387 proteins supported by a high level of biomolecules and nutrients in order to survive. Dr. Hubert Yockey, a physicist and information theorist at the University of California at Berkeley, who worked with Robert Oppenheimer on the Manhattan Project, tried to fabricate the most positive possible setting from which life could arise from non-life. He imagined a pool of pure amino acids assembled in the perfect environment. Give that pool a billion years, and at best, Yockey calculated it could produce a polypeptide chain of forty-nine amino acids.[131] Such a chain is one-eighth the size of a *single* protein.

Building on this, Dr. Jonathan Sarfati of the Victoria University of Wellington, New Zealand, calculated the possibility of life's simplest organism coming into being without help as one in 10^{4925}. And that's just to get the whole thing started. Considering that there are 10^{80} atoms in the universe and 10^{12} atomic interactions per second, and there have been 10^{18} seconds since the origin of the universe, Sarfati said only 10^{110} interactions are possible. He concluded that 10^{4925} is such a large number, it loses all meaning for us.[132] I may not be a biologist, but I can follow numbers. Life from nonliving chemicals is just not possible.

Species are retreating, not advancing.

Darwin's theory of evolution calls for small changes over time that result in large advances in life and complexity. One problem with this is that since the dawn of genetic studies, we have discovered that random changes never *add* genetic material to a species. In this sense, natural selection is not evolution; it is the reverse. Genes don't get added to a species; they may get "turned off" or mutated out. The essential microbe's genome is about 500,000 nucleotides. A human has three billion nucleotides. To change the former into the latter would require the addition of 2.5 billion nucleotides. Yet no one has ever observed speciation that involves the addition of a new biochemical pathway.[133]

Dr. John Sanford, geneticist from Cornell University, said that the process of mutation "is relentless and is destroying us, not creating us. We are heading for extinction, along with every other complex organism."[134] This is what the Second Law of Thermodynamics (Entropy) predicts.

"If it could be demonstrated that any complex organ existed, which could not possibly have been formed by numerous, successive, slight modifications, my theory would absolutely break down." Charles Darwin

---

Nature has too many irreducible complexities.

Over the last several decades, the relatively new science of microbiology has uncovered a level of complexity within living tissue that no one could have previously imagined. In every living creature and every living process within each creature are numerous sets of processes that could not have been built one small step at a time. Each part of the process of the reproduction of a cell, for instance, relies on simultaneous chemical or electromagnetic triggers from other apparatus within the cell that could not have come together except by careful design and could not have gotten started without an intentional "starter."

Imagine an internal combustion engine. Pistons can't fire without a chamber to confine them. That chamber must be filled with ignitable fuel, followed by a spark. The fuel must come from somewhere. After the explosion, the chamber must be vented before the process can repeat. The actual explosion is useless unless there is a transfer mechanism that captures the energy and puts it to work. Each of these parts and every step in the process *must* come together at once in order to create the moment necessary to generate energy. A piston sitting by itself, a chamber without a piston, a fuel injector without a chamber, fuel with no injector—each serves no purpose on its own.

The idea that just these few engine parts might all randomly assemble in a cohesive system is unthinkable, no matter how much time they have to get lucky. A partial combustion system serves no purpose on its own. In an organic system, such parts would be swept away through new mutations long before they had the chance to unite in an unanticipated practical function.

The chance that a random set of parts that serves no current purpose might survive long enough to become a digestive system or a kneecap requires more faith than believing that a Being exists who could create a digestive system or a kneecap. (What's more, it's counter to the Law of Evolution by Natural Selection. The fittest survive because they have effective and efficient parts.) Yet nature is brimming with systems that can't be reduced to simpler things. The complexity of nature is too well integrated to be accounted for by chance.

There is too much evidence for God to remove Him from the equation.

A reason, maybe the fundamental one, for believing in naturalistic evolution is to eliminate the need for the existence of God. In the first chapters of this book, we covered the implications of the existence of the universe, morals, personal experience, and the life of Jesus Christ as strong pointers to a Creator God.

William of Ockham was a fourteenth-century friar who studied logic and developed a principle that scientists have come to refer to as "Occam's Razor." (How they got from "Ockham" to "Occam" is a story for another day.) Ockham came up with the idea that *"More things should not be used than are necessary."* His exact phrase was *"Entia non sunt multiplicanda praeter necessitatem,"* but that's only really useful if you speak Latin. Occam's Razor dictates that when you encounter two potentially plausible explanations, choose the simpler one. In my opinion, *God* is a simpler and more elegant explanation than the drastic amount of chance and time required to build a world, much less an entire universe, with as many irreducible complexities as we find in ours.

Evolution has a negative effect on ethics.

How you see the world around you influences everything you feel and do. Darwin's theory of evolution has some stunning implications for the meaning of life and the value of humans, beasts, and all living things.

The Christian view is that humans are made in the image of God and, as such, have a sanctity about them that causes us to value life and treat others with care. God commissioned us to rule over the earth in Genesis 1:28, which means we have an obligation to treat it and its other inhabitants well.

The atheist view is that all life is random, the chance result of atoms and molecules coming together at a particular moment in time. This can be a depressing thought. Atheist Richard Dawkins wrote, "The universe we observe has . . . no design, no purpose, no evil and no good, nothing but blind, pitiless indifference. . . . DNA neither cares nor knows. DNA just is. And we dance to its music."[135] Evolutionary psychologist Susan Blackmore said, "In the end nothing matters. . . . If you really think about evolution and why we human beings are here, you have to come to the conclusion that we are here for absolutely no reason at all."[136] David Catchpoole fleshed this out practically when he wrote, "If random molecular rearrangements led to the first cellular life, which, purely by chance and time, eventually became people, then there is no basis for determining value for anything aside from the shifting sands of human opinion."[137]

You don't see it in print often, but the full title of Darwin's most famous book is *On the Origin of Species by Means of Natural Selection, or the Preservation of Favoured Races in the Struggle for Life*. You read it right. Darwin knew that the inescapable conclusion of his survival of the fittest theory is that "fitter" people have more value. In Darwin's second book, *The Descent of Man*, he prophesied, "At some future period, not very distant as measure by centuries, the civilized races of man will almost certainly exterminate, and replace, the savage races throughout the world."[138]

Applying Darwinian theory has resulted in tragic consequences. In the 1860s, Ernst Haeckel created a theory called *embryonic recapitulation*, which taught that "ontogeny recapitulates phylogeny"—basically, that the stages of evolution can be seen tracing the stages of development of a human embryo. Haeckel constructed a series of drawings supposedly showing that a human embryo has fish gills, then absorbs them and grows a temporary tail like a monkey. I remember seeing these drawings in my seventh-grade science book, even though the theory had been proven false decades earlier.

Believing that humans are just highly evolved molecular structures makes it easier to devalue life. Judge Harry Blackmun used "ontogeny recapitulates phylogeny" as part of his ruling in *Roe v. Wade,* a ruling that legalized abortion in the United States.

Haeckel evangelized Germany with the idea that some races are fitter than others. During the 1880s, German troops reduced the Herero people of southwest Africa from eighty thousand to fifteen thousand to make room for German settlers. During World War I, the first eugenics society was founded in Germany. It promoted the genetic purification of the races, an idea which justified the killing of six million Jews, Gypsies, handicapped people, and just about anyone else who caused inconveniences to the "master race" by Hitler and his friends during the second World War.

In the United States, eugenics was responsible for sterilizing seventy thousand people during the 1920s and 1930s, targeting the mentally retarded, the deaf and blind, people with epilepsy, criminals, and those with tuberculosis and syphilis.

In Russia, Joseph Stalin read *On the Origin of Species* as a thirteen-year-old. He told his friends, "God's not unjust, he doesn't actually exist. We've been deceived. If God existed, he'd have made the world more just. . . . I'll lend you a book and you'll see." He was talking about Darwin's *Origin*.[139] Stalin's Great Purge resulted in more than thirty million deaths.

In China, Mao Zedong's two favorite books were by Darwin and Aldous Huxley (also an evolutionist).[140] Mao's Cultural Revolution caused the deaths of forty to seventy million people. Mao's response was, "We have so many people; we can afford to lose a few."[141]

Belief that life is merely matter and we are here by chance has brought about something north of 130 million deaths by extermination or slaughter, to say nothing of the total by abortion and euthanasia.

If We Are Only Accidents . . .

C. S. Lewis wrote,

> If the solar system was brought about by acci-
> dental collision, then the appearance of organic
> life on this planet was also an accident, and the
> whole evolution of Man was an accident too. If
> so, then all our present thoughts are mere acci-
> dents—the accidental by-product of the move-
> ment of atoms. And this holds for the thoughts
> of the materialists and astronomers as well as
> for anyone else's. But if their thoughts—i.e., of
> Materialism and Astronomy—are merely acci-
> dental by-products, why should we believe them
> to be true? I see no reason for believing that one
> accident should be able to give me a correct ac-
> count of all the other accidents.[142]

Deciding for Yourself

In the Old Testament, Joshua led Israel during its conquest of
the land of Canaan. Toward the end of his life, he called the
people together and said to them,

> Now fear the LORD and serve him with all
> faithfulness. Throw away the gods your ances-
> tors worshiped beyond the Euphrates River and
> in Egypt, and serve the LORD. But if serving the
> LORD seems undesirable to you, then choose for
> yourselves this day whom you will serve. . . . But
> as for me and my household, we will serve the
> LORD. (Joshua 24:14–15)

On the surface, you could think that Joshua was calling people to a simple choice: "Pick a god, any god." But the choice of your god (or God) shapes how you see the world, what you value, and what you pursue, which makes the choice of your belief system the most important thing about you.

CHAPTER 34

CAN SCIENCE AND SCRIPTURE GET ALONG?

Do not treat prophecies with contempt but test them all; hold on to what is good, reject every kind of evil.

—1 Thessalonians 5:20–22

Is it possible to be a scientist and believe Scripture? Conversely, is it possible to be a person of faith and believe in science? There's a lot of friction between the two camps these days, but there doesn't have to be.

Blaise Pascal

During my (Hal's) junior year of high school, I took a course called "Advanced Topics in Mathematics." We learned a lot of formulas and equations that I've long since forgotten, but one thing I do remember is a report I almost flunked.

Our teacher wanted to inspire us to become mathematicians, so he assigned us each to write a biography on a great mathematician. We could choose any math guy we wanted. I had just learned about Pascal's Triangle,[143] so I thought, *Why not do a report on him?* I went to the library, checked out the few books available on his life, and went home to read.

Blaise Pascal had a profound influence on the science of probability. At age sixteen he wrote a treatise on projective geometry. At age nineteen he invented one of the first mechanical calculators. Later he added the hydraulic press, a primitive form of the roulette wheel, and the syringe. (Next time you get a flu shot, thank Pascal.) He's even credited with establishing the very first bus line, a mass transportation system to move people around Paris. I was truly impressed! Within the field of math, he had invented Pascal's Triangle and Pascal's Theorem. Then I turned the page and discovered Pascal's Wager.

Pascal's Wager argues that it's worth betting on and living as if God exists because if God exists, the upside is infinity, and if He doesn't, the downside is minimal. If you live for God and He doesn't exist, you may have lost a little pleasure and perhaps a little luxury. Whereas if God does exist and you follow Him, you reap an eternity in heaven and avoid an eternity in hell. An extension of this wager adds that even if you live for God and He doesn't exist, you will have lived a life that feels satisfying, generous, and fulfilling, which could far outweigh the pleasures and luxuries of the flesh anyway.

What does Pascal's Wager have to do with math? Unfortunately, not much. At age thirty-one, Pascal had become a Christian. My assignment was to research a mathematician, not a theologian. By accident, I had selected a devout Christian as my subject. As a typical teenager, I started the assignment twenty-four hours before it was due. By the time I found out Pascal had devoted the later years of his life to the pursuit of faith not science, the library was closed and I had no alternative but to report on this mathematician-turned-spiritualist and hope for the best. I said a quick prayer and turned in the paper. I don't remember what grade I received, but I think the teacher was merciful. At any rate, he didn't give me the F I was worried about.

Francis Collins

I have since discovered that Pascal's story is not unusual. A similar thing happened to Francis Collins not too long ago. Collins is a twenty-first-century geneticist and former agnostic. In his own words, "I became convinced that while many religious faiths had inspired interesting traditions of art and culture, they held no foundational truth."[144]

Then, at age twenty-six, Collins encountered the Moral Argument for the Existence of God (an argument we covered in chapter 3). He was exploring the evidences for God to confirm his atheism. He said,

> That now lay in ruins as the argument from the Moral Law (and many other issues) forced me to admit the plausibility of the God hypothesis. Agnosticism, which had seemed like a safe second-place haven, now loomed like the great cop-out it often is. Faith in God now seemed more rational than disbelief.[145]

Collins earned his doctorate in physics at Yale. He's the father of the Human Genome Project. His story of merging science and faith puts him in a long line of credible scientists.

The Scientist-Theists

Aristotle, a polytheist, is credited as the founder of empirical science. Ibn al-Haytham, a Muslim, refined the scientific process during what is known as "the Islamic Golden Age." Roger Bacon was the first Western scholar to promote inductive reasoning. Francis Bacon (no relation to Roger) refined the process further and is credited as inventing the modern scientific method. While not all of these men were Christians, all of them were men of faith who believed their research was exploring God's world.

Science and Scripture

When you think about it, science and faith are philosophical cousins. They both desire to discover and pursue truth. Science makes observations, collects data, and comes to conclusions. So does faith. Science begins with a set of presuppositions that must be accepted by faith before research is possible. Faith begins with a set of presuppositions that must be verified by logic, history, science, and/or revelation to be true.

Faith and science are a perfect match for each other. Science can tell us *how* a thing works but never *why* it works. Faith explains the *why*. Science uncovers facts. Faith lives and breathes values. The two need each other.

Many of science's greatest contributions have come from people of great faith.

"Science: The field of study that explains the workings of nature and the physical world that has evolved from an academic pursuit into a religion for atheists."
www.SarcasticPatriotDictionary.com

Scientists with Faith

King Solomon, of Old Testament fame, made impressive scientific contributions in his day: *"He spoke about plant life, from the cedar of Lebanon to the hyssop that grows out of walls. He also spoke about animals and birds, reptiles and fish"* (1 Kings 4:33).

At the head of the class of faith-filled scientists comes Sir Isaac Newton. Many consider Newton to be the greatest scientific mind of all time. Newton wrote several theological works and was fixated on the return of Christ. In his most important scientific work, the *Principia*, Newton wrote,

> This most beautiful system of the sun, planets, and comets, could only proceed from the counsel and dominion of an intelligent and powerful Being. . . . This Being governs all things, not as the soul of the world, but as Lord over all; and on account of his dominion he is wont to be called Lord God "pantokrator," or Universal Ruler.[146]

Right up there with Newton would be Johann Kepler. Kepler developed the laws of planetary motion and invented celestial mechanics. He was frequently heard saying (in German), "O God, I am thinking Thy thoughts after Thee." Kepler's most famous work was *Harmonies of the World*. It begins, "I commence a sacred discourse, a most true hymn to God the Founder, and I judge it to be piety . . . first to learn myself, and afterwards to teach others too, how great He is in wisdom, how great in power, and of what sort in goodness."[147]

Michael Faraday did seminal work in the fields of electromagnetism and electrolysis. Faraday wrote,

> Yet, even in earthly matters, I believe that "the invisible things of Him from the creation of the world are clearly seen, being understood by the things that are made, even His eternal power and Godhead," and I have never seen anything incompatible between those things of man which can be known by the spirit of man which is within him, and those higher things concerning his future, which he cannot know by that spirit.[148]

James Maxwell completed Faraday's work on the theory of electromagnetism in what is called "the second great unification of physics" (the first being the work of Newton). Maxwell wrote, "You may fly to the ends of the world and find no God but the Author of Salvation. You may search the Scriptures and not find a text to stop you in your explorations."[149]

The scientist/faith list includes Albrecht von Haller, the father of modern physiology; Gregor Mendel, the father of modern genetics; Georges Lemaitre, who coined the term "Big Bang"; and a thousand more. One can only conclude that, with the right perspective, science and faith go very well together, thank you.

Science Versus Scripture

On the other hand, friction often sets in between faith and science when a group of well-meaning Christians try to make the Bible say what it doesn't actually say.

In 1650, an Irish bishop named James Ussher published a book titled *Annales Veteris Testamenti, a prima mundi origine deducti.* If you were thinking of using that title, it's already taken. Ussher added up the years between births in the genealogies of the Old Testament and determined that the world came into existence on the evening of Saturday, October 22, 4004 BC. The idea of knowing the exact date of Creation so captivated people that they began including this piece of information in the marginal notes of study Bibles. Scripture never names or claims a Creation date, but well-meaning Christians bought into the 4004 BC time frame during the centuries that followed.

Another Christian misconception involved the idea that the sun revolves around the earth. Psalm 50:1 describes a daily rotation of the earth: *"The Mighty One, God, the LORD, speaks and summons the earth from the rising of the sun to where it sets."* Psalm 104:19 says, *"He made the moon to mark the seasons, and the sun knows when to go down.*" Christians didn't recognize that the psalms' composers were speaking *anthropocentrically*—that is, describing a phenomenon from a human perspective rather than recording a precise scientific description. The idea of a geocentric universe, where the sun revolves around the earth instead of vice versa, was so ingrained in the psyche of medieval church members that when Galileo proposed the opposite was true, the pope threatened to have him executed.

Well-meaning scientists have made the same mistake in reverse. Einstein was so smitten with the idea of a fixed universe that he made up a "cosmological constant" to keep from surrendering the idea because he knew a finite universe would strengthen the case for the existence of a Creator God.

More recently, scientists circulated findings that the human and chimpanzee genomes are 99 percent identical. This close match was claimed as evidence of evolution. Further review has shown that the match is closer to 70 percent.[150] Humans have entire gene families that are not found in chimps. Were evolution true, these genetic code lines would have had to somehow come into existence in an impossibly short period of evolutionary time.[151]

Science's Shortcoming

The challenge for science is that it is forever a work in progress. Much of what was understood as fact a hundred years ago within the scientific community has been proven inaccurate or inadequate today. There's a strong likelihood this will be true a hundred years from now as well.

Tensions often arise when two camps come at things from different angles. America's political system is a perfect example. What originally started as a disagreement between John Adams and Thomas Jefferson over federal jurisdiction versus states' rights sometimes breaks into a brawl between Democrats and

Republicans. Both parties are committed to a prosperous nation and the rule of law, but their divergent starting points have led to some embarrassingly heated discussions.

God's Principle

In 1 Thessalonians, the Apostle Paul encouraged the Thessalonians to pursue truth: *"Do not treat prophecies with contempt but test them all; hold on to what is good, reject every kind of evil"* (1 Thessalonians 5:20–22). Paul's focus was on prophecy, but the principle can also apply to other truth pursuits, such as science. In which case, the verse might be rewritten, "Test all the theories; hold on to ones that measure up, and reject those that don't." Men and women of faith have been doing just that for a long, long time.

Can science and Scripture get along? They are both authored and perfected by the same Source. When wise men seek God in the midst of their experiments, the world is almost always changed for the better.

CHAPTER 35

IF I'M CREATED BY GOD, CAN MY LIFE HAVE PURPOSE?

*"The Lord has made everything
for His own purposes."*

—Proverbs 16:4 NLT

Several years ago, I (Dan) was working as an announcer at a secular radio station in the Midwest. We were in a rather large city with a diverse population. I was live on the air, and one caller phoned in with a most unusual comment. He said that the only way to have purpose in life was through Jesus, and until the listeners took that step they would always be frustrated and living below their potential. He concluded by saying that the only way to understand our life purpose is to consult the One who created us. We were discussing a totally separate topic; however, I loved his boldness and perspective, and I wholeheartedly agreed with him.

I was flooded with different thoughts of how I should respond. I wanted to shift the entire program to the topic. I felt a sense of camaraderie with the caller who wanted my listeners to know God's purpose for their lives. I chose to affirm him and continue the show. But the caller hit a nerve with my listeners. I didn't have to shift the focus of the program; my listeners did it for me. It was amazing how many people wanted to know more about how to find their God-given purpose and direction for their life.

I suggested that if you were confused about the operation or purpose of a device, the best approach would be to consult the owner's manual. I added that the reason God gave us the Bible was to teach us what our life purpose is. I also advised, "If you want to know why a device was made, you should consult the Creator of the device." As an example, I said that I'd recently gone to an estate auction. While there, I stumbled across some strange-looking gadgets and gizmos. "Those gadgets looked strange to me, but the owner knew exactly what they were for," I said.

God has also fashioned you for a distinct purpose. He carefully crafted you to fulfill a part of His plan for all of creation. He planned who you would become and how long you would live. He designed your inquisitive mind. Even the way that you have wrestled with your own set of "God Questions" is a part of how God made you. No part of who you are is a mistake. The Bible reminds me that God "knew me before I was born and scheduled each day of my life before I began to breathe. Every day was recorded in His book!"[1] This is the amazing truth that comes from our owner's manual (the Bible).

God's plan also takes into consideration our unique talents and gifts. The Bible tells us *that we are God's workmanship created in Christ Jesus to do good works, which God prepared in advance that we should do."*[2] God does not simply leave His plan as a casual take-it-or-leave-it affair. He expects us to fully embrace it. He means business.

The apostle Paul said it this way: *"I plead with you to give your bodies to God. Let them be a living and holy sacrifice — the kind he will accept. When you think of what he has done for you, is this too much to ask?"*[3] Most of the time, we attempt to set our own life purpose. But we didn't create our life, so this doesn't always work well. Sometimes we live frustrated lives with little or no meaning or purpose. God created us, and He intends for us to grow and develop in areas we may have never considered. We will never know the possibilities that await us until we take Him up on His offer to guide us.

Regardless of who you are, God is serious about your life. Jesus is searching for people who will follow Him so that He can involve them in His eternal plan. Jesus said, *"All of us must quickly carry out the task assigned to us by the one who sent me."* 4 But you cannot carry out your life purpose until you decide to accept His plan for your life and Him as your Savior. Only then can you understand and summarize *God's purpose* for your life.

Summarize God's Purpose For You

Determine to take an action step: Write down a short statement of what you believe God's purpose is for your life. Even if you don't get it right at first, you are in the top 6% of Americans just because you have created a life purpose statement. Most people never take the time to establish this type of statement for their lives. Determine to make it a working statement; allow this to be a dynamic process, one that will be changed and adjusted as you grow and develop.

When you begin to consider God's purpose for your life, you may discover other related issues. Writing down your statement will force you to think about the direction your life is taking. It will also compel you to sort through what you value and hold most important. When you create a personal purpose statement, you also determine who or what will be the center of your life. This gives direction to your career, your finances, your family and just about everything else that matters to you.

Actually, whatever is at the center of your life is your god. All of our lives are centered on something—success, our spouse, money, ourselves—but is it the *best* center for our lives? The Bible says, *"Delight in the Lord, and he will give you the desires of your heart."* 5 God wants to be the center of your life!

How do you know when God is at the center of your life? When He is the center, you automatically align yourself to His way of operating and thinking. This has traditionally been called "worship." When God is not the center of our life, we worry. Worry is an indicator of a life out of alignment with God and His ways. As soon as we let God resume His rightful place at the center of our life, we will experience a quiet, calming peace, *"not a peace as the world gives."* [6] This new perspective will give purpose and hope. When you think about it, living on purpose is the only way to really live.

Take the time to pause at the close of this chapter and write a detailed life purpose statement. It is also helpful to summarize it into a brief repeatable phrase that you can use to guide and inspire you on a daily basis. When we remind ourselves daily that we are on a mission for the God of the universe, it will change our way of operating.

I have pared my life statement down to the sentence, *I want to live as a fully devoted follower of Christ, and allow this to influence me as a Christ-centered husband and father, to become more like Jesus in my actions, thoughts and dealings.* It's long, but it covers it all for me. Because it's all there in one sentence, I can use it as a reference point for my life. When I tend to venture off course, I can correct it based on what I have determined to be most important to me.

QUESTION #6
WHAT HAPPENS WHEN I DIE?

CHAPTER 36

WHAT WILL HEAVEN BE LIKE?

My Father's house has many rooms; if that were not so, would I have told you that I am going there to prepare a place for you? And if I go and prepare a place for you, I will come back and take you to be with me that you also may be where I am.

—John 14:2–3

When I (Hal) was a little guy, *The Wizard of Oz* was such an iconic movie that whenever it came on, my sisters and I were allowed to stay up and watch. One of the climactic moments in the film version comes when Dorothy and her friends are ushered into the great hall of the Wizard. Toto pulls back the curtain, and everyone gets to see the wizard face-to-face. The print version captures their emotions when it says, "And the next moment all of them were filled with wonder."

Everyone I know longs for that moment to happen in real life: to experience the wonder when the curtain of heaven is pulled back and we are allowed to see God face-to-face.

The sixth major question all of us have is "What happens when I die?" Over these last six chapters, I want to show you what the Bible says about the afterlife.

Television commercials sometimes picture heaven as a place where everyone sits on clouds, playing harps. If that is the case, I'd like to apply for time off for good behavior. One of the great myths of heaven is that we will become angels there. Every animal lover hopes his or her pet will be there. Will they? Will we see loved ones there? Will they recognize us?

People are often surprised to learn how much the Bible has to say about heaven. Even more, they are surprised to learn that the heaven our loved ones occupy now is not the heaven that will be with us forever. Theologians call the current place of those in God's presence "the intermediate state," or "the temporary heaven." One day this intermediate state will be replaced by the permanent dwelling of God's people called *"a new heaven and a new earth"* (Revelation 21:1). We'll read more about that throughout the next few chapters.

"Toto . . . tipped over the screen that stood in a corner. As it fell with a crash they looked that way, and the next moment all of them were filled with wonder." L. Frank Baum

---

What Is the Temporary Heaven Like?

Here are a few things you'll want to know about the current afterlife available to those who have died after trusting Jesus for salvation.

It is better by far.

The Apostle Paul, who through a miraculous set of circumstances described in 2 Corinthians 12:1–7, visited this next plane of existence. After experiencing it ever so briefly, he said, *"I desire to depart and be with Christ, which is better by far"* (Philippians 1:23).

It is a paradise.

Jesus called it this in Luke 23:43. *Paradise* is a word the Hebrews borrowed from the Persians. The Persians loved gardens. One of the Seven Wonders of the World was constructed by King Nebuchadnezzar for his wife, Amytis, who missed the lush green of her home in Media. Nebuchadnezzar built her the Hanging Gardens of Babylon. Cyrus, the Persian king who overthrew the Babylonians, also built elaborate gardens. The word *paradise* in Persian means "a walled garden." The present heaven is a place of paradise.

People there can see us here.

Hebrews 12:1 says that we are *"surrounded by such a great cloud of witnesses."* Somehow, those in heaven can see what we're doing now—which is both inspiring and a bit worrisome, isn't it?

People are made perfect there.

The writer of the book of Hebrews encouraged his audience by saying, *"You have come to Mount Zion, to the city of the living God, the heavenly Jerusalem. . . . You have come to God, the Judge of all, to the spirits of the righteous made perfect"* (Hebrews 12:22–23).

In Romans 6, the Apostle Paul spoke of the "old nature" inside of us and the "new nature" we receive when we come to Christ. In the next life, Christ followers will have their old nature extracted and be made morally perfect!

Two New Testament passages shed in-depth light on the current heaven. The first is the Parable of the Rich Man and Lazarus in Luke 16:19–31. The second is the description of the Martyrs Under the Altar in Revelation 6:9–11.

The Rich Man and Lazarus

Though the Parable of the Rich Man is a fictional story, some biblical scholars believe this parable describes supernatural reality because it is the only parable in which Jesus gave one of the characters a real name.

Jesus told it this way:

> There was a rich man who was dressed in purple and fine linen and lived in luxury every day. At his gate was laid a beggar named Lazarus, covered with sores and longing to eat what fell from the rich man's table. Even the dogs came and licked his sores.
>
> The time came when the beggar died and the angels carried him to Abraham's side. The rich man also died and was buried. In Hades, where he was in torment, he looked up and saw Abraham far away, with Lazarus by his side. So he called to him, "Father Abraham, have pity on me and send Lazarus to dip the tip of his finger in water and cool my tongue, because I am in agony in this fire."
>
> But Abraham replied, "Son, remember that in your lifetime you received your good things, while Lazarus received bad things, but now he is comforted here and you are in agony. And besides all this, between us and you a great chasm has been set in place, so that those who want to go from here to you cannot, nor can anyone cross over from there to us."
>
> He answered, "Then I beg you, father, send Lazarus to my family, for I have five brothers. Let him warn them, so that they will not also

> come to this place of torment."
>
> Abraham replied, "They have Moses and the Prophets; let them listen to them."
>
> "No, father Abraham," he said, "but if someone from the dead goes to them, they will repent."
>
> He said to him, "If they do not listen to Moses and the Prophets, they will not be convinced even if someone rises from the dead." (Luke 16:19–31)

If this story really is a window into the realities of the current heaven, five observations are worth noting:

(1) When Lazarus died, angels carried him to *"Abraham's side,"* which is a euphemism for heaven. When the rich man died, he went to Hades, which is a place of torment. Clearly, Jesus believed in a real heaven and a real hell.

(2) In heaven, Lazarus was with others. In hell, the rich man was alone. Lazarus experienced relationships. The rich man experienced isolation. I've heard people say, "I'd rather go to hell because that's where all the fun people will be." *Au contraire!* Hell is a place of solitude. When we reject God, we reject all that He offers, and one of God's great offerings is community. There will be no community in hell.

(3) The present heaven and hell are separated by a fixed chasm. Though the rich man was in agony, Lazarus was unable to help him because of this unbreachable gap. No one travels between heaven and hell.

(4) The rich man and Abraham reasoned, communicated, and remembered. If this parable truly is a reflection of reality, then people in the present heaven (as well as in the present hell) are fully aware of their circumstances and surroundings.

(5) In this story, the rich man had a tongue and Lazarus had fingers. This seems to indicate that those living in the

intermediate state have bodies. These may be *"spiritual"* bodies (1 Corinthians 15:44), but it's hard to imagine a truly "human" being without a brain and body. We'll see more of this in the second passage of Scripture: Revelation 6:9–11.

The Martyrs Under the Altar

The book of Revelation records what the Apostle John saw when he was taken to heaven in a mystical vision that enabled him to see the present heaven and the future outcome of life on planet Earth.

During his sojourn in the present heaven, John recorded this scene:

> I saw under the altar the souls of those who had been slain because of the word of God and the testimony they had maintained. They called out in a loud voice, "How long, Sovereign Lord, holy and true, until you judge the inhabitants of the earth and avenge our blood?" Then each of them was given a white robe, and they were told to wait a little longer, until the full number of their fellow servants, their brothers and sisters, were killed just as they had been. (Revelation 6:9–11)

These three little sentences are packed with insights about life on the other side of the grave. Here are a few:

(1) Just as in the Parable of the Rich Man, after death these people relocated to heaven.

(2) People in heaven are remembered by what they did on earth. These martyrs remember their life on earth and what happened to them there.

(3) These people have voices, which means they probably

have bodies. They're also wearing white robes. "Wearing" implies they have bodies on which to put these robes. Their voices are raised as one voice, so there's evidence of a unity of spirit among the peoples of heaven.

(4) They are fully conscious, rational, and aware. They aren't dazed or confused. These are fully functioning humans.

(5) They are free to ask God questions. This means they have free will and access to the Father.

(6) They know what's happening on earth. Somehow there is an ability to know what's happening here, at least on a grand scale, but possibly on a micro scale as well. If you've ever wondered if loved ones could be aware of the "doings" of earth, they're at least aware of the "big doings" and perhaps more.

(7) The people have feelings about what is happening on earth. They're passionate about justice and having wrongs rectified. It's fair to conjecture from this that they are able to *feel* in the same way we feel here and now.

(8) God answers their questions. Can you imagine living in a place where all your questions can be answered? That's an aspect of heaven most people long for.

(9) God tells them they will have to *"wait a little longer."* There is passage of time in heaven.

(10) They learn in heaven. It will take us an infinite amount of time to absorb an infinite amount of information, so we will always be learning.

(11) They're concerned about their *"brothers and sisters"* on earth. They have family ties to people now living.

(12) God knows the details of what is happening and will happen on earth, including all the suffering undergone by His children. The Voice of the Martyrs organization estimates that there are now 150,000 martyrs a year around the world. Four hundred people will die today for the cause of Christ, and four hundred tomorrow, and four hundred the day after that. God

knows them all. These have a very special place in the temporary heaven; they're as close to God as you can get: right under the altar in God's presence.

I once heard the story of an elderly lady who asked her pastor for a favor just before she died. "Please," she said, "put a fork in my hand and leave the coffin open during my funeral."

"Why?" asked her pastor.

"When I was a little girl, whenever my mother prepared a special dessert, while we were clearing our dishes, she would say, 'Save your fork, because the best part is yet to come!' I want everyone who views my body to know that the best is yet to come!"

CHAPTER 37

WHAT WILL HELL BE LIKE?

This is how it will be at the end of the age. The angels will come and separate the wicked from the righteous and throw them into the blazing furnace, where there will be weeping and gnashing of teeth.

—Matthew 13:49-50

If there's one God Question I'd like to avoid altogether, it's the question of hell. In some ways I wish we knew nothing of this horrible place. Sometimes I wish God had never created it.

Hell is a sobering reality. To ignore it is, at best, the definition of ignorance. To deny its existence is to deny there is free choice in this world. To try to wish it away has rash consequences. It would be like wishing you hadn't just hit your thumb with a hammer. You can pretend there is no throbbing at the end of your limb, but pretending doesn't change things nor does it treat the pain. The way to deal with this place of eternal anguish is to look it square in the eye and determine you are going to do everything you can to ensure that no one you love will go there.

What Is Hell?
The Bible uses four words to describe different aspects of hell. *Sheol* is the Hebrew word that is translated "the grave," "hell,"

and "the pit." The Greek equivalent is Hades. Both words refer to "the underworld." Hades was the gathering place of all souls[152] until Christ's death.

God hasn't given us architectural drawings for the layout of hell, but our best understanding is that Hades contains two or more chambers. The lower chamber is the place assigned to those awaiting judgment. The upper chamber is now vacant. It was for those awaiting Christ's once-for-all sacrifice on their behalf. Ephesians 4:8–9 describes the rescue of those in the upper chamber sometime between Good Friday evening and Easter Sunday morning: *"When he ascended on high, he took many captives and gave gifts to his people. (What does 'he ascended' mean except that he also descended to the lower, earthly regions?)"*

The Bible's third word for hell is *Gehenna*. Just like there is a temporary heaven that exists right now, there is also a temporary hell. Hades is the temporary hell; Gehenna is the permanent hell. In Luke 16:23, Jesus described the rich man *"in Hades, where he was in torment."* The torment of Gehenna will far exceed Hades.

"Almost everything that we know about hell in the New Testament comes from the lips of Jesus. I'm just guessing that in the economy of God, people wouldn't bear it from any other teacher." R. C. Sproul

---

One day, when the thousand years of the millennium are over,[153] *"death and Hades [will be] thrown into the lake of fire"* (Revelation 20:14), which is the permanent hell.

Gehenna is a *"place of judgment"* (1 Timothy 5:24), condemnation (see Matthew 23:33), and *"darkness"* (Matthew 8:12). It is a *"blazing furnace"* (Matthew 13:42), an *"eternal fire"* (Matthew 18:8), an *"unquenchable fire"* (Matthew 3:12), and a *"lake of fire"* (Revelation 20:14), with *"burning sulfur"* (Revelation 14:10). It is *"the Abyss"* (Revelation 9:1) and *"the second death"* (Revelation 20:14). Gehenna is a place of *"eternal punishment"* (Matthew 25:46) and *"everlasting destruction"* (2 Thessalonians 1:9).

The fourth word for hell is *Tartarus*. The ancient Greeks believed that Tartarus was located somewhere beneath Hades, or perhaps was its lowest chamber. In Greek mythology, Tartarus was reserved for the torture of the Titans. Peter borrowed the word *Tartarus* to describe the current prison of fallen angels: *"God did not spare angels when they sinned, but sent them to hell* [Tartarus], *putting them in chains of darkness to be held for judgment"* (2 Peter 2:4). Along with the devil himself, these demons will be cast into the lake of fire in Revelation 20:10.

Levels of Punishment

Many are surprised to learn that there will be degrees of reward in heaven and punishment in hell.

A startling scene comes during the final moments on our current earth. God will open His books and judge the dead *"according to what they had done as recorded in the books"* (Revelation 20:12). To picture how these varying degrees of judgment will be meted out, you'll have to use your imagination. The Bible doesn't say.

Jesus once stated that self-righteous men who took advantage of widows would *"be punished most severely"* (Luke 20:47). The greater the crime, the greater the punishment.

Jesus hinted at how guilt is measured in Luke 12:47–48: *"The servant who knows the master's will and does not get ready or does not do what the master wants will be beaten with many blows. But the one who does not know and does things deserving punishment will be beaten with few blows."* The more a person knows, the greater their responsibility for living it.

On another occasion, Jesus declared that the judgment on the cities of Tyre and Sidon would be *"more bearable"* than for those in cities where He had carefully proclaimed the truth (Matthew 11:22). The more you know, the greater your culpability.

Why We Hate Hell

We hate the very idea of hell because we have an instinctual desire to avoid going there. That desire extends to those we love. It even extends to people we have never met, because we know intuitively that they are made in the image of God. God loves people. Something inside of us wants good for all people, even if there is only a small amount of good in them.

We don't lament for demons because we know there is no good in them. We lament for our fellow humans because none of them has fallen fully to the place of complete depravity. We know that in heaven, the sinful nature will be removed from those who've trusted in Christ. Perhaps in hell, the vestiges of God's image will be erased from those who have rejected Him. This might be the case, because if not, there would be a small portion of something good residing in a place of complete lack-of-good, which seems logically impossible. If indeed any remains of God's image were wiped from the unrepentant, hell would become their natural home.

It sometimes helps me to remember that if God did not carry out eternal punishment, His justice would not be complete. I want to live in a universe where there is a God who is full of grace. Otherwise, there is no hope for anyone like me. I also want to live in a universe where there is a God who is completely just. Otherwise, no decision has real and true consequences.

A God who knows perfectly and creates a place like hell must see sin in much more stark and tragic terms than I do. When I realize this, I have to acknowledge that I am instructed by the existence of hell. By creating a place of horrible punishment, God is showing me that sin is more horrible than I want to admit.

How Can We Feel Joy in Heaven Knowing Someone We Love Is in Hell?

Romans 1:19–20 says that all people know the truth about God somewhere inside of them:

> *What may be known about God is plain to [all people], because God has made it plain to them. For since the creation of the world God's invisible qualities—his eternal power and divine nature—have been clearly seen, being understood from what has been made, so that people are without excuse.*

Once we reach heaven, we will be able to see just how clearly God revealed Himself to each of our friends and loved ones here on earth. In the presence of God, we will know without doubt that He was merciful and His final judgment was fair.

What Should I Do About Hell?

In Jesus's Parable of the Rich Man and Lazarus, the rich man undergoes an astonishing transformation. While on earth he didn't need God nor want anything to do with Him. Mere minutes in hell were enough to turn this self-made man into a radical evangelist. *"I beg you, father, send Lazarus to my family, for I have five brothers. Let him warn them, so that they will not also come to this place of torment"* (Luke 16:27–28).

As much as I dislike everything about hell, the reality of its existence drove me to leave the safe, comfortable community I

(Hal) was serving in and move to Oceanside, California, to start a church. For more than half my life now, I've prayed for people in my community to come to know Jesus. I do it at stoplights, in restaurants, and in grocery store lines. In moments when my mind is unoccupied, I look around at people and whisper, "Lord, I don't know the spiritual condition of that person, but I pray that they know You or will come to know You soon. If they don't know You, I pray that You'll use our church to introduce them to You."

Hell is a powerful motivator. It motivates us to diminish the sin in our lives. It motivates us to pray for people. And it motivates us to tell people about the means God has made available to enter heaven and avoid eternity's agony and suffering.

CHAPTER 38

WHAT WILL THE NEW EARTH BE LIKE?

See, I will create new heavens and a new earth. The former things will not be remembered, nor will they come to mind. But be glad and rejoice forever in what I will create.

—Isaiah 65:17–18

Every athlete has a day on his or her calendar that matters more than all the others. In football, it's the Super Bowl. In baseball, the World Series. Soccer has the World Cup; hockey, the Stanley Cup. From the opening day of training camp, every competitor dreams about making it to the one triumphant event where all the sweat, prayers, and tears will pay off. For Christians, that day will come on their first day in heaven.

What Will Heaven Be Like?

In chapter 31, we explored the present heaven. According to Revelation 20–22, that realm of existence will be replaced by the millennium, a period of *"a thousand years"* (Revelation 20:2), followed by the eternal state called *"a new heaven and a new earth"* (Revelation 21:1). The New Heaven and the New Earth have similarities to the present heaven and earth, with some significant upgrades.

The New Heaven

God knew we would have lots of questions about our eternal home, so He packed descriptions about it into every book of the Bible. We can't cover all of these in one or two chapters, so I'll give you the highlights.

One of the most thorough passages on heaven is found in Revelation 21:1–22:11. I encourage you to read it personally. The first thing you'll notice is that our present heaven and earth will pass away, being replaced with two new entities called *"a new heaven and a new earth"* (Revelation 21:1). The second thing you'll notice is that the habitation of humans will primarily be in a single city called *"the new Jerusalem"* (Revelation 21:2). This heavenly-city-come-to-earth may actually *be* the temporary heaven we learned about two chapters ago, currently located beyond the stars.

"Since where God dwells, there heaven is, we conclude that in the life to come heaven and earth will no longer be separated, as they are now, but will be merged. Believers will therefore continue to be in heaven as they continue to live on the new earth." Anthony Hoekema

The New Earth

At the close of the millennium, the Lord will bring the New Jerusalem to the New Earth. This city will be nothing short of amazing: opulent, built out of precious metals and gems, fit for the King of Kings. While royal cities of old were ornate, this city will surpass them all. Add the bonus that the New Jerusalem will house the throne of God itself, and you can see where the phrase "heaven on earth" came from.

People are sometimes surprised to learn that in the afterlife, we will actually live on earth. It will be a *new* earth, created by God to restore us to the perfect paradise He intended for us to experience from the beginning.

The New Jerusalem

The New Jerusalem will be *"laid out like a square, as long as it [is] wide"* and will span 12,000 stadia (1,400 miles) in length, width, and height (Revelation 21:16). Some picture it as a cube. More likely it is shaped like a perfect pyramid, its equilateral sides representing the three persons of the Trinity.

At 1,400 miles by 1,400 miles by 1,400 miles, the city will cover a territory the distance from Canada to Mexico and from the Appalachian Mountains to the far edge of the Mojave Desert. That's nearly two million square miles at the base, which is forty times the size of England and ten times as large as France or Germany. And that's just the ground level.

If this pyramid is built like a high rise, with each story twelve feet high, it could have as many as 600,000 stories. Billions of people could occupy this city and still enjoy a population density of several square miles per person. We won't be crowded, but we will all be living near each other.[154]

The 1,400-mile-length may be figurative. Either way, Revelation is communicating, "This is one massive city, where everyone will be close enough to find community and have enough space to experience privacy."

The River of Life

New Jerusalem has some unique geographic features. One of its great scenic wonders is *"the river of the water of life, as clear as crystal, flowing from the throne of God"* (Revelation 22:1). The Lamb of God (Jesus) occupies the throne of God. The River of Life flows down the center of the great street. New Jerusalem is the center of human life. Water is essential to human life. There will be an abundance of both water and life.

Modern cities like San Antonio and Spokane have realized that people love to congregate near water, so they've built attractive river walks. It's likely that the River of Life will have countless tributaries, with bustling river walk areas along many of its banks.

The city won't be flat. Water flows downward from the throne, which means God's throne will occupy the highest ground. Anyone wanting to visit God's throne need only follow the river upstream.

The Tree of Life

Another stunning feature of the city is its *"tree of life"* (Revelation 22:2). The tree stands on each side of the river. No living fauna compares to this tree. It's been in existence since Creation and bears fruit every month. It's a source of food, and it's a source of healing: *"The leaves of the tree are for the healing of the nations"* (Revelation 22:2).

God will use this tree to reconcile all factions who have fought, warred, or engendered bitter feelings toward each other. We will be reconciled by means of this tree, just as we were justified by the tree that became Christ's cross.

The *"tree of life"* is mentioned three times in Genesis and four times in Revelation. According to Revelation 2:7, this tree currently grows in the temporary heaven. This is the same tree God intended for our original parents, Adam and Eve, to eat from and live forever. For all eternity, all redeemed humanity will enjoy its fruit.

The prophet Ezekiel proclaimed, *"Fruit trees of all kinds will grow on both banks of the river. Their leaves will not wither, nor will their fruit fail. Every month they will bear fruit, because the water from the sanctuary flows to them. Their fruit will serve for food and their leaves for healing"* (Ezekiel 47:12).

Some scholars believe the tree of life is a collective reference. It may refer to many trees, or perhaps to a tree with shoots underground that surface all over the city. My father has a eucalyptus grove in his front yard. Stroll through it and you'll think you're in the midst of a mini-forest of trees, whereas actually this grove is all one tree with an extensive root system that sends up shafts all over the yard. I believe the tree of life will be similar, which explains how it can grow on both sides of the river.

The Country
Hebrews 11:14–16 assures us there will be countryside as well as city. The New Earth will have spacious outdoors. The ecology of the country will be as impressive as the architecture inside the city!

The Mountains
Revelation 21:10 pictures *"a mountain great and high."* Not *the* mountain, but *a* mountain, which means there will be more than one mountain on the New Earth. There will be soaring peaks to appreciate and climb. Image the slopes, lakes, waterfalls, and meadows these mountains will provide. Recreational opportunities will abound in the re-creation!

The Sea
Revelation 21:1 says, *"There was no longer any sea."* To ancient peoples, the ocean represented things that were cold, dark, and dangerous. When God originally created the seas, He pronounced them good. The Curse had a devastating effect on all creation; thousands of microscopic organisms became harmful to animal and plant life. As a countermeasure, the sea needed to become salty, neutralizing these life-threatening bacteria and preventing our oceans from becoming gigantic, toxic cesspools.

In the New Earth, all bacterium will be restored to its pre-Fall state. It could be that Revelation's description of "no more sea" means the oceans will become fresh water, like lakes, and much calmer than they are now. Imagine a lake as large as the Pacific, which you can drink from and swim in at the same time.

Our Hearts Confirm Heaven

In my role as pastor, I'm privy to the secret hopes and dreams of people from all walks of life. I've yet to meet anyone who feels fully settled in this world. Even in the moments of our greatest joy, there seems to be something missing or incomplete about the lives we lead on earth. Philosophers say this inner longing for something more is a subtle proof that we were made for something more. We never have felt, and never will feel, fully satisfied and settled here because this world is only a temporary home. The New Earth is the true home for which we were fashioned and formed. Columbus and his men kissed the ground when they came ashore in the new world. I suspect we will do the same when we finally set foot on the New Earth!

CHAPTER 39

WHAT WILL MY LIFE BE LIKE THEN?

"What no eye has seen, what no ear has heard, and what no human mind has conceived"—the things God has prepared for those who love him— these are the things God has revealed to us by his Spirit.
—1 Corinthians 2:9–10

The New Earth is the place we long for. Last chapter we explored what that new world will be like. But what will *we* be like? What will we do there? What will we feel and think? Will we have friends? Know loved ones? Find meaningful things to do? Have a purpose that fulfills us?

A Personal Experience at the Start

The New Heaven and the New Earth will begin with the passing away of the old creation, the descent of the New Jerusalem, and the angelic proclamation that *"God's dwelling place is now among the people"* (Revelation 21:3). At that moment, the Lord will begin personally ministering to every inhabitant of His New Creation. He'll wipe every tear-stained face as He empathizes with the traumas we endured from our previous life on earth. Once we've had that personal experience, *"there will be no more death or mourning or crying or pain, for the old order of things has passed away"* (Revelation 21:4).

Some believe that once God wipes our tears, we will never cry again. I don't see it that way. Tears are a significant part of the human experience, and we will still be humans. I don't cry often, but some of my most significant moments, like the births and weddings of my children and the births of their children, have included tears. The "no more crying" reference in the verse above is grouped in with "no more death or mourning or pain." All of these are associated with negative experiences. There is a difference between crying because of sorrow and shedding "happy tears."

Bodies

If you'd like a bodily makeover, get ready. We will receive "resurrection bodies" similar to the resurrected body Jesus lived in during His forty post-resurrection days on earth.[155] There is no physical description of how Christ's body changed between Good Friday and Easter Sunday, but there are plenty of hints about what that body was like.

The first person Jesus appeared to on Resurrection morning was Mary Magdalene.[156] She recognized Him only after He called her by name. Later that day, He appeared to two disciples on the road to Emmaus. Initially, neither of them knew who He was.[157] However, as He said the blessing over their meal together that evening, *"their eyes were opened and they recognized him"* (Luke 24:31).

Your resurrection body will be similar to your current body, but not identical. At thirty-year high school reunions, friends recognize each other, but it sometimes takes a little context to jar their memories. The Bible's great description of our current bodies versus our new bodies comes in 1 Corinthians 15. The Apostle Paul said,

> *The sun has one kind of splendor, the moon another and the stars another; and star differs from star in splendor. So will it be with the resurrection of the dead. The body that is sown is perishable, it is raised imperishable; it is sown in dishonor, it is raised in glory; it is sown in weakness, it is raised in power; it is sown a natural body, it is raised a spiritual body.* (1 Corinthians 15:41–44)

Like everything in heaven, your resurrection body will be *"better by far"* than your current model (Philippians 1:23). After His resurrection, Jesus ate like a normal human,[158] but He also walked through a wall,[159] something I'd very much like to do one day!

Housing

If you've dreamed of a new home, be encouraged. On His final night before the Crucifixion, Jesus told the disciples, *"My Father's house has many rooms . . . I am going there to prepare a place for you"* (John 14:2). It could be that your initial personal time with Jesus will include a tour of your new home. The word *room* is also translated "dwelling place" or "mansion." Your new digs may or may not be attached to other people's homes. We don't really know. The Lord is creating perfect spaces for each of us based on His knowledge of our personal preferences. Since that's the case, I think I'll be overlooking water on one side, mountains on another, with grass and trees and family nearby. The good news is, God knows us better than we know ourselves, so when you see your new home, it will be more perfectly suited to you than you could even imagine.

Time

If you're worried about being bored, don't be. For years I pictured heaven as somehow "outside of time." But considering that the tree of life bears fruit *"every month"* (Revelation 22:2); that God will show us the incomparable riches of His grace throughout *"the coming ages"* (Ephesians 2:7); and that mankind will come and bow down before God *"from one Sabbath to another"* (Isaiah 66:23), our experience in heaven will clearly be "inside" of time. Heaven will have things to work toward, events to spur us on to greater attainments, and meaningful activities to look forward to.

Foods

If you're worried that your stomach will be useless in heaven, don't be. Jesus told His disciples, *"I confer on you a kingdom, just as my Father conferred one on me, so that you may eat and drink at my table in my kingdom"* (Luke 22:29–30). In Revelation, He said, *"To the one who is victorious, I will give the right to eat from the tree of life"* (Revelation 2:7). With a lack of pestilence and only cooperative weather patterns, imagine the fruits and vegetables the land will produce!

Not only will we eat, but the ground will be full of rich nutrients and minerals. We'll enjoy more flavorful foods with more acute taste buds. Several of Jesus's parables speak of future banquets. The *"wedding supper of the Lamb"* will be a huge feast (Revelation 19:9). I'm not sure if calories will disappear, but our resurrected bodies will come with enhanced metabolism and enhanced self-restraint.

One disappointing piece of news on the food front is that

we may all be vegetarians. Isaiah 11:6–9 says,

> *The wolf will live with the lamb,*
> *the leopard will lie down with the goat,*
> *the calf and the lion and the yearling together;*
> *and a little child will lead them.*
> *The cow will feed with the bear,*
> *their young will lie down together,*
> *and the lion will eat straw like the ox.*
> *The infant will play near the cobra's den,*
> *and the young child will put its hand into*
> *the viper's nest.*
> *They will neither harm nor destroy*
> *on all my holy mountain,*
> *for the earth will be filled with the knowledge*
> *of the LORD.*

That's quite a number of carnivores living side by side with their former prey.

It's likely that the eating of meat didn't begin until after the Flood. Adam and Eve had a meat-free diet. I love steak, so I'm doing my best to eat my fill now, because we may not get another chance once the New Creation is ushered in.

Animals

If you're an animal lover, no doubt you noticed all the livestock listed in the previous passage. If wolves and lambs will be on the New Earth, so will dogs, cats, and other pets.

Angels

If you've dreamed of becoming an angel, you won't. Humans don't become angels when we get to heaven. In some sense, we may be superior to them though. First Corinthians 6:3 says that *"we will judge angels."*

Marriage

If you've wondered about marriage in heaven, Jesus said, *"At the resurrection people will neither marry nor be given in marriage; they will be like the angels in heaven"* (Matthew 22:30). Instead of being married to another person, we will all be married to the Lamb. We will be the *"bride"*; He will be the Bridegroom (Revelation 19:7; 22:17).

Marriage on earth is preparation for a close relationship with God one day. Nothing will take away from the rich relationships you may have had with your spouse and family members here on earth. After all, all sin and tarnish will be worn away there. The perfect marriage you've always longed for will be had in your relationship with the Savior. As a result of that relationship, all other relationships will be better than they are today!

"Travel has no longer any charm for me. I have seen all the foreign countries I want to except heaven and hell and I have only a vague curiosity about one of those." Mark Twain

---

Knowledge

If you've wondered about what you will know or understand one day, the Apostle Paul said, *"Now we see only a reflection as in a mirror; then we shall see face to face. Now I know in part; then I shall know fully, even as I am fully known"* (1 Corinthians 13:12). In heaven we will see things more clearly and know much more than we do now, yet we will never know everything. Only God is omniscient. What you can't see from the English text of this verse is that there are two different words for "know" in the sentence. The first "know" is *ginosko*. It means "know" in the sense of "learning." In heaven we will be learning fully. The second "know," translated "fully known," is *epiginosko*, which means "to know extensively." Only God knows fully (*epiginosko*). We will continue to learn each day, forever.

Work

If you've wondered whether you'll have a job in heaven, remember that work is a good thing. The only bad work is work we don't like. Work can give a sense of purpose, accomplishment, and worth. Adam worked the Garden of Eden before the Fall. Jesus said, *"My Father is always at his work to this very day"* (John 5:17).

In heaven you'll be given significant assignments for meaningful tasks that keep you growing and enhance the lives of others. These assignments will be doled out based on your performance in this present life.

The Best Promise

The Bible says, *"Our present sufferings are not worth comparing with the glory that will be revealed in us"* (Romans 8:18). I think it's impossible to imagine today what that glory will be like in the future. There will be glory revealed in us, like an athlete who has achieved her best; or a scholar, scientist, or artist who has done his best—maybe even more.

The word *glory* (*doxa*) means "light, brilliance, or radiance." We sometimes say of a bride or a pregnant woman, "She's *glowing*." Medieval artists painted the saints in heaven with halos as an attempt to convey a glow, or *glory*, that radiated from these heavenly humans. You won't have a halo, but it's likely you will have a magnificence and resonance about you.

One of my favorite quotes is by the Oxford scholar C. S. Lewis. He once told an audience,

> It may be possible for each to think too much
> of his own potential glory hereafter; it is hardly

possible for him to think too often or too deep-
ly about that of his neighbour. The load, or
weight, or burden of my neighbour's glory [is
a] load so heavy that only humility can carry
it, and the backs of the proud will be broken.
It is a serious thing to live in a society of pos-
sible gods and goddesses, to remember that the
dullest and most uninteresting person you can
talk to may one day be a creature which . . . you
would be strongly tempted to worship.[160]

Potential

Will anyone be perfect in heaven? Only God. The rest of us,
though immortal, will remain finite and ever-progressing toward
perfection. Only God is fully actualized. The rest of us will always
have some potential yet to be achieved. Yet, when heaven opens
for us, we'll be set—or reset—at a level based on things that are
judged important by God and not necessarily important by our
world. This reset will make us leaps and bounds more mature and
complete than we could ever hope to become in this life.

Altogether Better

The author of Hebrews once described a number of impressive
men and women of God. He called them *"a great cloud of wit-*
nesses" to our present situation (Hebrews 12:1). He wrote,

All these people were still living by faith when
they died. They did not receive the things prom-
ised; they only saw them and welcomed them
from a distance, admitting that they were for-
eigners and strangers on earth. People who say
such things show that they are looking for a

country of their own. If they had been thinking of the country they had left, they would have had opportunity to return. Instead, they were longing for a better country—a heavenly one. Therefore God is not ashamed to be called their God, for he has prepared a city for them. (Hebrews 11:13–16)

The New Heaven and New Earth is a better country, by far, with a better city, by far. You and I will be better people, by far, and better off there, by far. This place is not a concept, and it is not ethereal. Heaven is real. And real people—all those who express their trust in Christ—will one day be there. Throughout history, those who have understood this fantastic future have longed for it with the anticipation of a bride or groom waiting for their wedding day.

CHAPTER 40

HOW SHOULD I PREPARE FOR HEAVEN?

Store up for yourselves treasures in heaven, where moths and vermin do not destroy, and where thieves do not break in and steal.
—Matthew 6:20

At New Song, we have a class on imperatives that I (Hal) teach to all new members of the church. Toward the end of the class, we spend some time talking about eternity. I draw a six-inch line on the whiteboard and say, "This represents the span of my life. I don't smoke, drink, or chew, and my wife won't let me buy a motorcycle, so I'll probably live ninety years or so." I draw a second line all the way across the whiteboard. As I'm drawing it I say, "Stop me when I get to the length of eternity."

When I reach the end of the board, someone always yells out, "Keep going!" I continue an imaginary line across the length of the classroom. As I get to the corner, someone shouts, "Keep going!" again. I walk to the next wall, then the next wall, then the next wall. When I get back to the whiteboard, they say, "Keep going!" one more time.

"What if I were to draw a line all the way around the room? Would that be long enough for eternity?" I ask.

"No, eternity never stops."

I come back to my original six-inch line and mark an X on it. I tell them, "This X represents a vacation my wife and I are going to take next summer. We're going to spend a week in the Rocky Mountains because we love the Rockies. We love the Rockies so much, we're investing everything we have to build a mansion for the week we'll be spending there."

I face the group and say, "What would you call me if I were to tell you that we love the Rockies so much, we are going to spend everything we have on building this mansion so we can spend a week there?"

For the last twenty years the class has always answered the same way. "We'd call you a fool." I don't blame them. I'd call me that too. Anyone would be a fool to invest the efforts of their whole life on a short portion of their lifespan.

One reason God spent so much time telling us about eternity was so we could prepare for it. Scripture is packed with descriptions of heaven because its Maker wants you to know about it and prepare for it. This world is not your final destination—not even close. This world is *preparation* for your final destination.

There Will Be Treasures in Heaven

During Jesus's Sermon on the Mount, He cautioned,

> *Do not store up for yourselves treasures on earth, where moths and vermin destroy, and where thieves break in and steal. But store up for yourselves treasures in heaven, where moths and vermin do not destroy, and where thieves do not break in and steal. For where your treasure is, there your heart will be also.* (Matthew 6:19–21)

You'll never see a hearse pulling a trailer because it's impossible to take your worldly treasures with you. The good news is, you can send them on ahead!

The Apostle Paul was one of the smartest and most driven men in history. He spent time thinking carefully about how to make the most of his one-and-only life and concluded that the solution was to focus his efforts on eternity: *"I press on toward the goal to win the prize for which God has called me heavenward in Christ Jesus"* (Philippians 3:14). Paul knew that there were prizes to be won in heaven.

"I must make it the main object of life to press on to that other country and to help others to do the same." C. S. Lewis

---

How to Get to Heaven

Heaven is attained by the merits of another. We gain entrance there not because of deeds we have done but because of what Jesus did on our behalf. He laid down His life so that *"whoever believes in him shall not perish but have eternal life"* (John 3:16).

How to Get Rewards

Once we reach heaven, however, there are rewards for things we've done on earth. These rewards are based on our efforts to advance God's kingdom. In 1 Corinthians 3, the Apostle Paul talked about building Christ's Church:

> If anyone builds on this foundation using gold, silver, costly stones, wood, hay or straw, their work will be shown for what it is, because the Day will bring it to light. It will be revealed

with fire, and the fire will test the quality of each person's work. If what has been built survives, the builder will receive a reward. If it is burned up, the builder will suffer loss but yet will be saved—even though only as one escaping through the flames. (verses 12–15)

Like building a mansion for a week in the Rockies, it is possible for a person to expend all their efforts on their life here on earth and have nothing left to show for it on the New Earth.

In the Parable of the Talents, Jesus told a story of three men entrusted with portions of their master's money. Two of them doubled the amounts they'd been given. The third one didn't even try to earn anything with his entrustment. To the first two men, the master said, *"Well done, good and faithful servant!"* He put each of them in charge of even more, saying, *"Come and share your master's happiness!"* (Matthew 25:21, 23).

To the third man, he said, *"You wicked, lazy servant!"* He took away what had been entrusted and threw him *"outside, into the darkness"* (Matthew 25:26, 30). It's a stark tale with a poignant application: Jesus is offering significant incentives to those who will join Him in the cause of building the kingdom of God.

What Rewards Are Available?

It cannot be overstated that salvation, which is the entrance pass to heaven, is a free gift. Ephesians 2:8–9 says, *"For it is by grace you have been saved, through faith—and this is not from yourselves, it is the gift of God—not by works, so that no one can boast."* Once we've experienced grace, gratitude motivates us to serve the Lord. Because of all that God has given and forgiven us, we shouldn't need incentives to serve, but He gives them anyway. Throughout Scripture, the Lord outlines numerous rewards for serving Him. These rewards are literally out of this world.

Here are a few of them:

Good Words

Imagine locking eyes with Jesus for the very first time and hearing Him say to you, *"Well done, good and faithful servant"* (Matthew 25:21). I think you'd remember those words and that moment for all of eternity.

Good Jobs

In the Parable of the Ten Minas, the master says to his servant, *"Because you have been trustworthy in a very small matter, take charge of ten cities"* (Luke 19:17). To another servant he says, *"Take charge of five cities"* (Luke 19:19). In Matthew 19:28, Jesus tells the disciples, *"At the renewal of all things, when the Son of Man sits on his glorious throne, you who have followed me will also sit on twelve thrones, judging the twelve tribes of Israel."* In a sense, this life is a job interview for a permanent position in the next life. Prove faithful here and you will be rewarded with a great job there. Serving well in a significant ministry responsibility in your local church just might earn you a mayorship or judgeship in heaven.

A Good Seat

In Revelation 3:21, Jesus said, *"To the one who is victorious, I will give the right to sit with me on my throne, just as I was victorious and sat down with my Father on his throne."* When I was a youngster, my father read the newspaper in his big chair every night before dinner. I was so glad to have him home that I would come into the living room and watch him read. Sometimes he would lower his newspaper, inch to one side of the chair, and pat the empty space, inviting me to sit beside him. I still remember the scent of his aftershave and the smell of the newspaper as I scooted up next to him. If one of my sisters came into the room, I would feel a secret sense of pride sitting there with our dad. Imagine what it would feel like in the throne room of heaven if, in the midst of mass worship, the Father scooted to one side of His throne and invited you to sit next to Him while the multitudes sang His praises!

Good Gifts

Throughout the New Testament, faithful servants of God earn five special gifts. These gifts are called "crowns," hinting that they may bring special honors with them. There will be times when all those who are worshiping will bow and remove their crowns, laying them at the Lord's feet as an offering.[161] I feel awkward about the idea of wearing a crown, but I get excited by the idea of having something significant to lay at God's feet!

Over the centuries, theologians have labeled these five crowns: the Crown of Righteousness, the Crown Imperishable, the Crown of Life, the Crown of Rejoicing, and the Crown of Glory. The crowns are each awarded for a different type of service, so it may be possible to earn more than one.

The Crown of Righteousness is given to all those who long for Jesus's appearing.[162] The Crown Imperishable comes to those who work hard for the cause of Christ.[163] The Crown of Life is awarded to those who are martyred for the cause of Christ.[164] Those who lead others to Christ are given the Crown of Rejoicing.[165] Those who pastor a group of God's people well receive the Crown of Glory.[166]

Good Friends

In Luke 16, Jesus told the story of a shrewd manager in order to make this point: *"Use worldly wealth to gain friends for yourselves, so that when it is gone, you will be welcomed into eternal dwellings"* (verse 9). I know of a man who donated $400,000 to pay for the air conditioners in his church. He reasoned that if people felt comfortable during the church's services, they would be more likely to listen well. And if they listened well, they would be more likely to respond to an invitation to become Christ followers. Over the years, that church has seen thousands come to Christ. Imagine this man's reception one day as he's invited into the eternal homes of each of those grateful people.

Hidden Manna

Revelation 2:17 mentions three rewards that are cryptic enough to have me stumped. In that verse Jesus said, *"To the one who is victorious, I will give some of the hidden manna. I will also give that person a white stone with a new name written on it, known only to the one who receives it."*

Manna was the miraculous food God provided for the Israelites while they were in the wilderness.[167] Orthodox Jews believe that manna will be the food served in heaven. I don't think that's what this is. Members of my church sometimes give my wife and me homemade bread or cookies at Christmas time. We're grateful for these gifts, but I suspect the *"hidden manna"* is more than a tasty morsel. In the Old Testament, manna materialized every day. What if this is a new gift from God every morning? Manna seems to have been a food that contained all the nutrients an Israelite would need for the day. Maybe the hidden manna is something unusual that sustains you in special ways. Manna came directly from God. You couldn't get it any other way. Might this be something that can be obtained only because of the favor of God? We don't know now. But someday we will!

A White Stone

In certain cultures, when a jury reached a verdict, they would deliver a black stone if the person was guilty or a white stone if he was acquitted. In other cultures, the winner of a race would be given a special white stone that would gain him entrance into exclusive parties and places. We can speculate on what the *"white stone"* is, but I wonder if part of God's delight will be in handing out prizes we can't guess at or anticipate. Maybe this and/or the hidden manna will be such prizes.

A New Name

The *"new name"* in Revelation 2:17 will be a special name, known only to God and its recipient. If you've ever had someone you admire bestow a secret name or title on you, you know how good that feels. A few months after I started my first official church job, an older gentleman named Jack took me to breakfast one morning. Jack spent a full five minutes telling me all the good things he saw in my life. He concluded with, "Hal, you're a winner." That was thirty years ago. Sometimes when I'm discouraged, I replay that memory and think, *Things aren't that bad. Jack thinks I'm a winner.* If God gives you a new name, I'll bet you will replay the moment of bestowal often in eternity!

One reason eternal rewards are so significant is because they are *eternal.* The Apostle Peter said they can never *"perish, spoil or fade"* (1 Peter 1:4). God is such a good God that I imagine He will devise awards for us to earn once we get to heaven, but these eight types of rewards can only be earned while on earth.

Christmas Eve

A faithful elderly Englishman named H. S. Laird was close to death when his son asked, "Dad, how are you feeling?"

Laird answered, "Son, I feel like a little boy on Christmas Eve."

That's the way God wants us to anticipate heaven: a Christmas Day stocked with eternal presents!

Life on earth can contain some exhilarating moments. Once it's done, life only gets better for those who have trusted Christ. Heaven is a place of unspeakable joy, and a place with eternal rewards!

Gaining What Can't Be Lost

While in college, Jim Elliot wrote in his journal, "He is no fool who gives that which he cannot keep to gain that which he cannot lose."[168] After college, Elliot became a missionary to the Auca Indians, a South American tribe that had never heard the name of Jesus. The tribesmen martyred Jim and four colleagues as these men were trying to earn their trust. He gave his life (something he could not keep) to help others gain eternal life (something he and they could not lose). Months later, Jim's widow Elisabeth was accepted by the Aucas, and she led many of them to faith in Christ, including the man who put a spear in the chest of her husband. I'm eager to see the rewards Jim has gained for losing his life for the Aucas, aren't you?

CHAPTER 41

WHAT DO I DO NOW?

From everyone who has been given much, much will be demanded; and from the one who has been entrusted with much, much more will be asked.

—Luke 12:48

Every spring, young people march down aisles, receiving applause and diplomas. In unison they shift tassels from one side of their mortarboards to the other. A benediction is said, hats go flying, hugs are exchanged, and newly minted graduates drive home with a nagging thought: *What do I do now?* For years they've pursued education. Now it's time to put it into practice. Where do you start? Is there a five-point checklist somewhere that explains how to navigate real life?

The list may be out there, but I haven't heard of it. I have done a lot of thinking, though, about what to do with the God Question answers you've been acquiring. Here are six suggestions to help you live out what you've learned:

1. Receive Christ

If you haven't already done so, today can be your day of salvation. The Bible says, *"To all who did receive him, to those who believed in his name, he gave the right to become children of God"* (John 1:12). I encourage you to pray this simple prayer out loud: *"Lord Jesus, I believe in You. I receive You now into my life.*

I want to be a Christian. Forgive me for the things I have done wrong. Lead me from now to eternity."

If you've sincerely prayed that prayer, all the promises of God and all the truths of this book will be applied to your life, starting now! The Bible says, *"There is rejoicing in the presence of the angels of God over one sinner who repents"* (Luke 15:10). There's a party going on in the unseen realm, and your name is on the "Welcome Home!" banner.

2. Share What You've Learned

Admit it. You now know a fair amount about God, Jesus, the Bible, religions, the problem of pain, the origins of the universe, and what comes after the grave. If you've read this whole book, you know more on these crucial topics than I did the day I graduated from seminary. Don't let it go to your head, but do let it go to your heart. Thank God for what you now know about Him. And be ready to politely, appropriately, and confidently share your answers with others who need them.

Good things happen when you share what you've learned. People grow, and you grow even more! The Apostle Paul told his friends, *"Entrust [what you have learned] to reliable people who will also be qualified to teach others"* (2 Timothy 2:2). Invite a few friends to join you in a six-week walk through these chapters and Bible discussions. If you can afford it, buy copies of the book for the people you want to share your answers with.

3. Look for Opportunities

You are a carrier, and God knows you are a carrier! You carry in your head many practical and encouraging answers to life's most important questions. Expect that He will put people in your path who need answers. At the same time, remember that no one was ever argued into heaven. God says, *"Always be prepared to give an answer to everyone who asks you to give the reason for the hope that you have. But do this with gentleness and respect, keeping a clear conscience"* (1 Peter 3:15–16).

4. Pray for Open Doors

The Apostle Paul knew that he had answers, so he asked his friends to help him find people who needed them. *"Pray for us,"* he said, *"that God may open a door for our message, so that we may proclaim the mystery of Christ"* (Colossians 4:3).

"Life is so much more than good intentions. What you hope for sustains you, what you think about directs you, but what you do defines you." Hal Seed

---

5. It's Okay to Not Know Everything

When a friend asks you a God Question, it's okay to say, "I don't know." People respect honesty more than pretense. Say, "That's a good question! I don't know the answer right now, but I know there is a good answer. Can I do a little research and get back to you?" Then flip to the table of contents, reread the appropriate chapter, and get back to them.

6. Loan This Book

If you're worried you won't be able to express your answer well, that's okay too. I wrote this book hoping to help you. And I wrote it hoping to help you help others. Sometimes the simplest way to help a friend is to bookmark a page and hand them the book.

The last paragraph of a book is usually reserved for an ending. I didn't write one here because I'm praying this will actually be a beginning for you. God bless you as you use what you've learned to live with greater understanding in this world and to win friends who will welcome you into eternal dwellings!

CHAPTER 42
WHAT HAPPENS TO ME WHEN I DIE?

"...and the dust returns to the ground it came from,and the spirit returns to God who gave it."

—Ecclesiastes 12:7

There comes a point in each person's life when we ask on some dark night, "Is this life all there is?" It's a valid and profound question, and one we don't often share. Instead, we ponder it privately in our hearts.

With the rise of spirituality in the late 1990s and early 2000s, interest in life after death is at an all-time high. Bookstores offer dozens of titles that describe afterlife scenarios. Anecdotes recounting mysterious out-of-body experiences have become commonplace. Interestingly, most of the stories we hear have happy endings. But some near-death stories describe a much darker encounter.

In his research on near-death encounters, Dr. Maurice Rawlings found that just about half of the people who experience out-of-body encounters have a vision of hell instead of a vision of heaven. These darker stories don't usually make the press, but they are equally significant. Rawlings found that many people were so unsettled by their near-death encounter that they did not want to talk about it. In fact, they struggled to deal with the experience at all.

Our interest in the afterlife says some positive things about our culture. First, it says we're thinking about what comes next. Thinking precedes preparation; that's a good thing. Second, if these documented experiences are true, it indicates that there *is* life after death. This is good news, but it leads to something that worries me. People I know and love plan to spend eternity in heaven, but they are not necessarily consulting with *God* about those plans. In fact, some are leaving "the God of heaven" out of their lives altogether.

In the 1970s and 80s, many baby-boomers acted as if, by ignoring aging, they could perhaps also ignore their mortality. But in the end, Mark Twain had it right: There are only two things we can be sure of in this life, *death and taxes*. Death is no respecter of persons, regardless of how wealthy, old, beautiful or powerful we are. None of us can avoid it.

According to the Bible, death is the dividing line between this life and "eternity." Compared to eternity, this life is like a fading flower or withering grass.[9] Smart investors put their assets into the thing that will last.

Jesus: The Eternal Expert

Jesus spoke more about eternity than did all of the other Biblical writers combined. He is, after all, the only One able to speak about eternity from personal experience. He also personally knows the joy of being with the Father in a complete relationship in the eternal realms even before the beginning of time. The Bible says that after his crucifixion, Jesus "...descended to the lower, earthly regions."[10] Jesus experienced the devastating loneliness and isolation of being separated from the Father during and just after his death on the cross. Jesus is the *only* expert on the subject of eternity. Jesus spoke warnings about living well, so that we would be prepared for eternity. He taught about this topic from a position of love. Jesus taught that we have a loving Father who desires an eternal relationship with us and a fulfillment of the purpose to which we have been called—to glorify Him. Jesus said, *"I desire that they ... may be with me ... and that they may behold my glory."* [11]

Jesus often taught about heaven and hell. His references to heaven were not so much about palatial cities of grandeur and beauty, but as a place of being in relationship with Him and His Father.

Two Kinds of Death

The Bible teaches that there are two kinds of death: The first is a physical death; the second death is an eternal, spiritual death. Jesus cautioned us to be more concerned about the second death than the first. He warns, *"Do not be afraid of those who kill the body but cannot kill the soul. Rather, be afraid of the one who can destroy both soul and body in hell."* [12]

Jesus' teachings on the subject of hell were graphic and visual. He made reference to a place near the ancient city of Jerusalem known as Gehenna. It was located outside the city wall and was the place where the city's trash would burn and smolder without ever being extinguished. From the vantage point of Gehenna, you would probably be able to look up and see the activities of life in the city. However, since no one could scale the slippery, spring-fed, mossy rock walls around the city, this point of view would most likely make you feel trapped and lonely. So from the perspective of Gehenna, one would require no further explanation of how unpleasant and isolated hell will be. By the reference, Jesus was indicating that those who choose to live separately from God in the physical life will remain lonely and separated from Him in the afterlife.

Jesus further illustrates the nature of eternity in a story of two very different men. The first owned much, and the second owned little. The wealthy man was possessed by his possessions and was concerned about finding pleasure in life. The poor man ate the breadcrumbs from the rich man's table. At the time, it was customary for wealthy people to wipe their hands on bread like napkins and then dispose of the bread by tossing it from the table. The poor would come after the meal and eat the bread that the wealthy had tossed away.

Eventually, both rich and poor men die and are faced with two very different eternities. The poor man, because of his priorities, had inherited God's eternity. By no means does this story imply that Jesus condemns riches; however, he does caution us not to become so busy accumulating things that we have no time for God. Jesus also distinguishes between the place of eternal comfort and the place of eternal torment and separation, and He clearly reminds us that after we die, there are only two alternatives.

In our popular culture where everything is relative, many people do not accept this teaching of Jesus. People prefer to believe that heaven exists, but they deny the existence of hell, or they assume it is simply a temporary place of penance. Many who believe in heaven cut-and-paste it together with mythological icons such as clouds, angel wings and harps.

The Choice is Yours

Jesus' teaching about the nature of heaven and hell was not intended to scare us; it was meant to teach us how to live. Imagine you and I were driving and saw a sign warning that a bridge ahead was unsafe. Would we speed up, ignoring the people and signs trying to stop us from driving across the bridge? If we refused to stop despite the advice, we would be responsible for our own deaths. God has warned us that this life and the decisions we make in this life are serious matters. We will go to one of two destinies in eternity, and we are each fully responsible for our eternal destination. Author C.S. Lewis said, "Hell is locked from the inside. The residents of hell have chosen the outcome of hell with intention and clarity."[13]

The benefit of accepting Christ as our Savior is that we can live without fear. Jesus told us that we do not know the time of His return, so we should live our lives prepared for it. He said, "*No one knows about that day or hour, not even the angels in heaven, nor the Son, but only the Father.*" (Matthew 24:36)

Because we do not know when that day will come, we certainly do not know if we can afford to wait to make a decision to follow Christ. None of us can be certain when the end of our life will be. Jesus tells us to prepare now.

God has taken considerable steps to ensure that we have an eternal choice. Jesus came to offer us the gift of eternal life in heaven. We must turn from our ways and yield to Him to redeem the offer. I invite you to take this all-important step now. Simply ask God to come into your life through the presence of the Holy Spirit. It is as simple as pausing now, bowing your head and whispering the prayer that can change your eternity:

Jesus, I know that You are the answer I've been looking for. I will follow You, and I receive You as my life director. Thank You for saving me and making me perfect. Thank you for preparing a place for me to be with You in heaven. In Your name, I pray. Amen.

If you have taken this all-important step, I want to rejoice with you and welcome you to the family of God and to your eternal destiny! The next step is to tell someone about your decision. This is the beginning of a life with God and His family.

THE GOD QUESTIONS
SMALL GROUP
DISCUSSION
GUIDES

QUESTION #1

IS GOD REAL?
BIBLE STUDY

Connect with Each Other

- Have you ever been someplace in the world that was so beautiful you had to stop and stare? Where were you? What thoughts went through your head as you looked around?

If we're honest, at one point or another, most of us have asked the question, "Is God real?" It's easy to start wondering about God when you see some of the amazing places, creatures, and people this world holds.

Explore the Bible

- Open a Bible to Psalm 19 and read verses 1–4 aloud.
- What aspects of the world does the psalmist (David) mention specifically?
- What other aspects of the world have you noticed and been amazed by?
- In verse 2, when David said the heavens "pour forth speech" and "reveal knowledge," what do you think they're saying?
- In verse 4, David said it's as if the creation has "words." How far did he say these words reach?
- Read Psalm 139:13–16 aloud.
- How involved is God in the creation of each human being?

Apply the Bible

- Based on these passages, how should we look at the world around us?
- What should our response be when we see beauty?
- What should our response be when we see broken people and things?
- Based on Psalm 19 and Psalm 139, how does it make you feel to know that God made you to be a part of the world that brings Him glory?

Discover the Whole Picture

- In chapter 1, we mentally put the entire universe in a circle as we looked at one of the evidences for the existence of God. What's inside the circle? What's outside the circle? How does this point us toward the existence of God?

- In chapter 2, we heard how a Pepsi can and a banana point us toward God's existence. How? Can someone explain the argument?

- In chapter 3, it says, "We all have a moral standard that is higher than ourselves." Raise your hand if you have ever done something you knew was wrong. How can understanding this moral code point us to understanding God's existence?

- In chapter 4, we heard about how Jesus claimed to be God. Jean-Jacques Rousseau said, "Yes, if the life and death of Socrates are those of a philosopher, the life and death of Jesus Christ are those of a God." Do you agree or disagree?

- In chapter 5, we heard about how personal experiences can point us to God. Share about a personal experience you had of either doubting or encountering God.

- In chapter 6, we explored the nature of faith. Hebrews 11:1 says, *"Now faith is confidence in what we hope for and assurance about what we do not see."* In what ways this week have you had to express confidence in what you hope for or assurance about what you do not see?

Grab a Takeaway

- What doubts or questions do you still have about the existence of God? What would you need to understand or have answered in order to believe in Him?

- How does understanding the evidences for the existence of God motivate you to tell others about Him?

Pray Together

- How can we be praying for each other this week? Share an area you'd like prayer for this week.

IS THE BIBLE TRUE? BIBLE STUDY

Connect with Each Other

- What was your first encounter with the Bible? Where were you? What were your perceptions of the Bible at that time?

Whether you have been familiar with the Bible for a long time or it's kind of a foreign book to you, the Bible has so much to say to us in our daily lives. So, as we explore the idea of "Is the Bible True?" let's begin by seeing what it says about itself.

Explore the Bible

- Open a Bible to Proverbs 30 and read verses 5–6 aloud.
- How does the author describe God's words?
- Why should this be a comfort to us?
- Share a time you saw God's *"flawless"* words affect a decision you made in your life.
- Based on Proverbs 30:5, do you think we should value some biblical books over others? Why or why not?
- What does verse 6 say we should *not* do? Why?
- Read Revelation 22:18–19 aloud.
- Again, here at the end of the Bible, we hear a similar warning. What did John, the author of Revelation, say will happen to anyone who adds to the words of that scroll?
- What are some things/people/shows/websites in our society that people give equal authority to the Bible?

Apply the Bible

- How does it make you feel knowing that every word of God's is *"flawless"*?
- How does knowing the Bible is *"flawless"* affect the way you respond to opinions you hear from people and read on the Internet?

Discover the Whole Picture

- In chapter 8 we explored who wrote the books of the Bible. Why is it important to know that the Bible's authors were either prophets or apostles, or someone with direct linkage to one or the other?

- In chapter 9's reading, we heard that the Bible is unique in its continuity, circulation, translation, survival, and teaching. Which one of these explanations is most interesting to you? Can you explain it to the group?

- In chapter 10's reading, we explored how the Bible was transmitted. What were some of the extreme steps scribe groups took to protect the accuracy of the transmissions?

- In chapter 11's reading, we heard some of the proven scientific claims the Bible makes. What surprised you in this chapter?

- At the very beginning of chapter 12's reading, we learned a number of words the Bible uses to describe itself (i.e., active, authoritative, enduring, flawless, good, instructive, perfect, powerful, revelatory, trustworthy, etc.). Which of these things do you need the most right now in your life?

- In chapter 13's reading, we talked about inspiration—how God gave His words to human writers. In what ways do we see God's creativity in how the Bible was written?

Grab a Takeaway

- How has learning more about the Bible's writers, translations, accuracy, and teaching motivated you to read more of it?

- If someone were to ask you, "Why do you trust what the Bible says?" how would you answer them?

Pray Together

- How can we be praying for each other this week? Share an area you'd like prayer for this week.

QUESTION #3

DO ALL ROADS LEAD TO HEAVEN? BIBLE STUDY

Connect with Each Other

- Do you have any friends/co-workers who practice a different religion from you? Raise your hand if you've ever gotten into a religious conversation with them. What do they believe about the afterlife?

The vast majority of the world is religious. With so many differing beliefs, it's normal to wonder, *"Do all roads lead to heaven?"* Let's explore what the Bible says about Jesus and what eternity looks like from the Christian perspective.

Explore the Bible

- Open a Bible to John 14 and read verse 6 aloud.
- What are the three words Jesus used to describe Himself?
- Which of these three words stands out to you the most? Why?
- What did Jesus say is the only way to the Father?
- Read Matthew 7:13–14 aloud.
- What analogy did Jesus use when explaining eternal life to His disciples?
- Read Acts 4:12 aloud.
- What did Peter say was *"found in no one else"*?

- What does "salvation" mean? (Consider having a different person look up each verse to read aloud: Luke 1:77; Romans 5:9; Ephesians 1:13; 1 Thessalonians 5:9; Titus 2:11; 1 Peter 1:5; 1 Peter 3:18.)

Apply the Bible

- If you had to define salvation in one sentence (or two) based on the verses above, what would your definition be?

- Based on John 14:6 and Matthew 7:13–14, what should our response be to those who ask, "What does the Bible say about how to get to heaven?"

Discover the Whole Picture

- In chapter 15, we chewed on the idea that "The wonder is not 'Why is there only one way?' It's 'Why is there any way at all?'" Can someone explain this to the group? Do you agree or disagree?

- In chapter 16's reading, we looked at what Muslims believe. What are the Five Pillars of Islam, and how are they similar and dissimilar from the Christian faith?

- Chapter 17 is all about Hindus. Based on the chapter, can someone explain the Hindu idea of the afterlife?

- In chapter 18's reading, we explored the Buddhist faith. What is the Eightfold Path? Can someone explain it to the group?

- In chapter 19, in the discussion of the Christian faith, we looked at Four Solutions. What are these solutions, and which solution does Christianity fall under?

- Chapter 20 has a discussion of various religious beliefs. Choose one and explain it to the group.

Grab a Takeaway

- If you have a friend or co-worker who holds one of the religious beliefs we discussed, what is one way you can engage them in conversation this week?

- If someone were to ask you, "Do you believe there's only one way to heaven?" how would you answer them?

Pray Together

- How can we be praying for each other this week? Share an area you'd like prayer for this week.

QUESTION #4

HOW CAN A GOOD GOD ALLOW SUFFERING? BIBLE STUDY

Connect with Each Other

- What is something you saw on the news recently that made you sad about the state of our world? If you could have written the story of that event, what would you have made happen differently?

When we look around, it isn't hard to see that the world we live in has trouble, sorrow, disaster, and heartbreak. Somehow, we know this just isn't right. But if God is so good, why is there so much bad in the world? Today, we're going to explore what the Bible says as well as some Hard Answers, Head Answers, and Heart Answers to this question.

Explore the Bible

- Open a Bible and read Genesis 2:15 and all of Genesis 3 aloud.
- What was the one command given to Adam (Genesis 2:15)?
- What did Adam and Eve do (Genesis 3:6)?
- What did God say would be the curses visited upon females as a result of this sin (Genesis 3:16)?
- What did God say would be the curses visited upon males as a result of this sin (Genesis 3:17–19, 23)?

- As you can see, a huge change took place when Adam and Eve sinned. What was the world like before they ate the fruit? What was it like after they ate the fruit?

- Read Romans 8:22 aloud.

- Who or what does this verse say has been *"groaning as in the pains of childbirth"*? What do you think that means?

- How have you seen that our world is not as it should be lately? Can you share an example from your personal life?

- Read 2 Peter 3:8–13 aloud.

- In verse 9, what does the Apostle Peter say the Lord is *not*? What does he say the Lord is instead?

- What is going to happen on *"the day of the Lord"* (2 Peter 3:10, 12–13)?

- Where will people live after *"the day of the Lord"* (2 Peter 3:13)?

- Why has God not brought about *"the day of the Lord"* yet (2 Peter 3:9)?

Apply the Bible
- Based on Genesis 3 and Romans 8:22, what should we remember when we see the world in decay?

- Based on 2 Peter 3:9, what should we do with this slowness or this time God has given us here on earth before the day of the Lord comes? Is there anything holding you back from repenting of your sins and trusting in Jesus?

Discover the Whole Picture
- At the beginning of chapter 22, we saw three common options people use to explain why there's evil in the

world. Can someone describe Option #1? Option #2? Option #3? What's the alternative explanation?

- In chapter 23's reading, how is "free will" defined? What are the two kinds of evil we see in our world?

- In chapter 24, what are five ways God uses trials for good in our lives?

- Chapter 25 suggests that there are two kinds of answers—logic-based answers and feeling-based answers. What kind of answers do you need, personally, with regard to suffering?

- In chapter 26, we learned that we are in the middle of the story. What will happen in Act III of the story (Revelation 21:4)?

- Chapter 27 talks about hell. What is the purpose of hell?

Grab a Takeaway

- If you could write a letter to God, what personal hardships or grief would you ask Him about? What do you think He would say in return?

- How can you focus on Act III of the story this week when you feel down?

Pray Together

- How can we be praying for each other this week? Share an area you'd like prayer for this week.

WHICH IS RIGHT: EVOLUTION OR CREATION? BIBLE STUDY

Connect with Each Other

- What's the best thing you've ever made with your own two hands? What made you proud of it?

The world around us is so fascinating that it's natural to ask, "Where did this all come from?" You have probably heard the debate between evolution and creation. Today, we're going to explore what the Bible says and see if we can gain some clarity on "Which is right?"

Explore the Bible

- Open a Bible and read Genesis 1 aloud.
- According to Genesis 1, what was the world like before Creation (Genesis 1:2)?

- What happened on Day One of Creation (Genesis 1:3–5)? On Day Two (Genesis 1:6–8)? On Day Three (Genesis 1:9–13)? On Day Four (Genesis 1:14–19)? On Day Five (Genesis 1:20–23)? On Day Six (Genesis 1:24–31)?

- When God saw all that He had made, what did He say about it (Genesis 1:31)?

- If you could have watched one of the days of Creation take place, which one would you have liked to see? Why?

Apply the Bible

- How does reading the Creation account make you want to care for God's creation around you?

- Compare the Bible's Creation account to your understanding of evolution. What questions do you still have that would help you clarify, "Which is right—evolution or creation?"

Discover the Whole Picture

- In chapter 29, we saw four options in the debate: Natural Selection, Theistic Evolution, Intelligent Design, and Biblical Creationism. Can someone explain each of these to the group?

- In chapter 30's reading, we discussed the Big Bang theory. How does the Big Bang work or not work within a finite universe?

- In chapter 31, we asked the question, "Who made God?" Was God created or not? Explain.

- Chapter 32 suggests that science confirms the Bible. How? Can someone explain this argument to the group?

- In chapter 33, we studied evolution. What are some of the shortcomings of the theory of evolution?

- Chapter 34 is about science and the Bible. Why are there often such heated arguments between naturalistic scientists and people of faith? Which scientist did you most enjoy reading about in this chapter?

Grab a Takeaway

- How does the level of detail and accuracy of the Creation account alter or improve your view of science?

- Does what you've read about creation versus evolution this week influence how you want to live in any way? If so, how?

Pray Together

- How can we be praying for each other this week? Share an area you'd like prayer for this week.

WHAT HAPPENS WHEN I DIE? BIBLE STUDY

Connect with Each Other

- What are some common pictures of heaven we see in the media or culture today? Do you think these are accurate?

The media and people around us portray heaven a certain way, and it's normal to wonder what heaven is really like. Today we're going to explore the question, "What will heaven be like?" by looking at what the last two chapters of the Bible say about heaven and eternity.

Explore the Bible

- Open a Bible and read Revelation 21 and Revelation 22:1–5 aloud.

- According to Revelation 21:1, what's going to be new and what's going to pass away?

- What will happen to death, pain, and the like (Revelation 21:4)?

- How is the alternative to heaven described (Revelation 21:8)?

- What does the New Jerusalem look like (Revelation 21:10–21; 22:1–5)?

- What is *not* in the New Jerusalem (Revelation 21:23–25, 27; 22:3, 5)?

- Who is allowed to enter this perfect place (Revelation 21:27)?

- Who is *not* allowed to enter this perfect place (Revelation 21:8, 27)?

- If you could take any living person with you to walk around in this place for just one day, who would you bring with you? Why?

Apply the Bible

- How does picturing what heaven is like make you want to go there?

- How does it make you feel to know that if you have put your faith in Jesus, you will be in this place someday?

- Knowing that *"only those whose names are written in the Lamb's book of life"* (Revelation 21:27) may enter, who do you need to talk to or pray for this week?

Discover the Whole Picture

- At the beginning of chapter 36, we heard the Parable of the Rich Man and Lazarus. Based on the book, what are some observations we can make about the temporary heaven from this parable?

- In chapter 37, we discussed what hell is like. What are some of the things the Bible says about hell?

- Chapter 38 is all about the New Heaven, the New Earth, and the New Jerusalem. What are some of the key physical descriptions the Bible gives about these places?

- Chapter 39 is about what our personal experience will be like in heaven. What are some of the similarities and differences between our lives here and our lives in heaven?

- Chapter 40 describes how to prepare for heaven. It lists actions to take here that will result in rewards there. List some of the rewards available in heaven. Which ones would you most like to achieve?

- In chapter 41, we discussed what to do now. What do *you* need to do now to respond to everything you've learned about heaven this week?

Grab a Takeaway

- How does knowing about heaven give you hope in this life?

- Who do you think would be a good person for you to lend your copy of the book to?

- What study will this group begin together next week?

Pray Together

- How can we be praying for each other this week? Share an area you'd like prayer for this week.

NOTES

QUESTION #1: IS GOD REAL?

CHAPTER 2: WHERE DID THE WORLD COME FROM? (PART 2)

1   William Lane Craig, *Reasonable Faith: Christian Truth and Apologetics* (Wheaton, IL: Crossway, 1994), 84.

2   Quoted in *Heroes of History* (W. Frankford, IL: Caleb, 1992), 434.

3   This analogy is adapted from Ray Comfort, *God Doesn't Believe in Atheists* (South Plainfield, NJ: Bridge Publishing, 1993), 15–17.

CHAPTER 4: WHO IS JESUS?

4   Jesus made verbal claims to be both Messiah and God. And He made many deliberate nonverbal demonstrations that He was God. See, for instance, Matthew 12:6; 16:16–17; 21:15–16; 23:37; 28:18; Mark 2:1–2; 10:18; 14:53–65; John 4:25–26; 8:58–59.

5   This argument has been popularized by Josh McDowell, *A Ready Defense* (Nashville: Thomas Nelson, 1993), 241–245.

6   C. S. Lewis, *Mere Christianity* (New York: MacMillan, 1960), 40–41.

7   See John 19:1.

8   Dr. C. Truman Davis, quoted in McDowell, *A Ready Defense*, 222, cites the following expert description: "The heavy whip is brought down with full force again and again across [a person's] shoulders, back and legs. . . . The small balls of lead first produce large, deep bruises, which are broken open by subsequent blows. Finally the skin of the back is hanging in long ribbons and the entire area is an unrecognizable mass of torn, bleeding tissue. When it is determined by the centurion in charge that the prisoner is near death, the beating is finally stopped."

9   See John 19:2.

10 See John 19:17.

11 See Mark 15:21.

12 See John 19:34.

13 See Matthew 27:60; John 19:41.

14 See John 19:39.

15 McDowell, *A Ready Defense*, 225.

16 See Mark 15:46.

17 See Matthew 27:65.

18 A Roman guard unit consisted of sixteen men; each was trained to protect the six square feet in front of him. Together they were expected to hold thirty-six yards against an entire battalion. Four men were stationed directly in front of the object they were protecting, with the other twelve asleep in a fan shape in front of them, with heads pointed in. To pierce this defense, thieves would first have to walk over the sleeping guards, then confront the four fully armed soldiers. Every four hours a fresh set of four men were awakened and rotated to the direct-guard position.

19 See Matthew 27:66.

20 See Mark 16:3; John 20:11.

21 See Mark 16:11; John 20:13, 25.

22 See Matthew 27:5.

23 McDowell, *A Ready Defense*, 231.

24 McDowell, *A Ready Defense*, 234. Note: Some people choose to believe that the guards fell asleep or went AWOL. The penalty for either offense was death.

25 See John 20:6–7.

26 See Matthew 28:1–6; Mark 16:1–6; Luke 24:1–6; John 20:1–8.

27 See Mark 16:1; Luke 24:13–18, 36–39; John 20:10–20, 26–28; 1 Corinthians 15:3–6.

CHAPTER 6: IS THERE ANY PROOF I CAN TOUCH?

28 See Matthew 22:37.

29 See Ecclesiastes 3:11.

QUESTION #2: IS THE BIBLE TRUE?

CHAPTER 8: WHERE DID THE BIBLE COME FROM?

30 See Joshua 24:26.

31 See 1 Samuel 10:5; 19:20.

32   See 1 Chronicles 29:29.
33   See 2 Chronicles 9:29; 13:22.
34   See 2 Chronicles 20:34.
35   See 2 Chronicles 32:32.
36   See 2 Chronicles 33:19.
37   Norman Geisler and William Nix, *From God to Us* (Chicago: Moody, 1974), 82–83.
38   Josephus, *Against Apion*, I. 8.
39   The Talmud records, "After the latter prophets Haggai, Zechariah, and Malachi, the Holy Spirit departed from Israel."
40   The writings done during this period in Israel are a collection of fifteen books known as "the Apocrypha." They were adopted as inspired by the Catholic Church at the Council of Trent in 1546, after the onset of the Protestant Reformation, but have never been recognized as such by the Protestant, Anglican, or Orthodox churches.
41   Paul wrote Romans through Philemon, thirteen out of the New Testament's twenty-seven books.

CHAPTER 9: HOW IS THE BIBLE DIFFERENT FROM OTHER BOOKS?

42   http://www.greatsite.com/ancient-rare-bible-leaves/gutenberg-1455-leaf.html.
43   Dr. Steve Kumar with Dr. Jonathan Sarfati, *Christianity for Skeptics* (Creation Book Publishers, 2012), 100.
44   http://www.gospelcom.net/ibs/aboutibs/historical.php.
45   Josh McDowell, *Evidence That Demands a Verdict* (San Bernadino, CA: Campus Crusade for Christ, 1972), 20–26.
46   http://www.gospelcom.net/ibs/aboutibs/historical.php.
47   http://www.biblesociety.org/index2.htm.
48   https://en.wikipedia.org/wiki/Bible_translations.
49   Bernard Ramm, *Protestant Christian Evidences* (Chicago: Moody, 1957), quoted in Josh McDowell, *A Ready Defense* (Nashville: Thomas Nelson, 1993), 30.
50   John Warwick Montgomery, *History of Christianity* (Downers Grove, IL: InterVarsity, 1971), 29, quoted in McDowell, *A Ready Defense*, 30.
51   McDowell, *A Ready Defense*, 30.
52   For specific prophecies, consult www.godandscience.org.
53   William Albright, *Recent Discoveries in Bible Lands* (New York: Funk & Wagnalls, 1955), 70ff.

CHAPTER 10: WHAT ABOUT ERRORS IN THE BIBLE?

54   Christian Apologetics & Research Ministry, www.carm.org.
55   Bruce M. Metzger, *Chapters in the History of New Testament Textual Criticism* (Grand Rapids, MI: Eerdmans, 1964), 144.
56   Ken Boa and Larry Moody, *I'm Glad You Asked* (Colorado Springs, CO: Victor Books, 1994), 92.

CHAPTER 11: IS THE BIBLE TRUE?

57   Hugh Ross, www.reasons.org.
58   Consult www.reasons.org for more extensive descriptions.
59   See Ecclesiastes 1:9; 3:14–15.
60   See Job 36:27–29.
61   See Ecclesiastes 1:7; Isaiah 55:10.
62   See Job 26:7; 38:31–33. (Note: According to Dr. Ross, "All other star groups visible to the naked eye are unbound, with the possible exception of the Hyades.")
63   See Proverbs 15:30; 16:24; 17:22.
64   See Leviticus 13:45–46.
65   See Numbers 19; Deuteronomy 23:12–13.
66   Roy Abraham Varghese, ed., *The Intellectuals Speak Out About God* (Lake Bluff, IL: Regnery Gateway, 1984), 21.
67   Donald J. Wiseman, "Archaeological Confirmation of the Old Testament," in *Revelation and the Bible*, Carl F. H. Henry, ed. (Grand Rapids, MI: Baker, 1958), 301–302.
68   See 1 Kings 16:23.
69   See 2 Kings 10:36.
70   See 2 Chronicles 32:2–9.
71   See 2 Kings 24:10; Ken Boa and Larry Moody, *I'm Glad You Asked* (Colorado Springs, CO: Victor Books, 1994), 97.
72   John Garstang, *Joshua Judges* (Grand Rapids, MI: Kregel, 1931), quoted in McDowell,

    Evidence, 71.

73 See John 5:1–15.

74 F. F. Bruce, "Archaeological Confirmation of the New Testament," quoted in McDowell, *Evidence*, 75.

75 See Luke 2:1–2.

76 See Luke 2:2.

77 See Acts 14:6.

78 See Luke 3:1.

79 Joseph P. Free, *Archaeology and Bible History* (Wheaton, IL: Scripture Press, 1969), 1.

80 See Isaiah 27–32.

81 http://ragz-international.com/chaldeansneb.htm.

82 http://joseph_berrigan.tripod.com/ancientbabylon/id34.html.

83 John Ankerberg and John Weldon, *Ready with an Answer* (Eugene, OR: Harvest House, 1997), 248.

84 Erwin W. Lutzer, *Seven Reasons Why You Can Trust the Bible* (Chicago: Moody, 1998), 98.

85 http://www.iclnet.org/pub/resources/text/rtg/rtg-evid/rtgevd04.txt.

86

Prophecy:	Fulfillment:
Born of a woman, Gen. 3:15	Matt. 1:20; Gal. 4:4
Born of a virgin, Isa. 7:14	Matt. 1:18; Luke 1:26–35
Called, "The Son of God," Ps. 2:7	Matt. 3:17; 14:33; 16:16; 26:63
Seed of Abraham, Gen. 22:18	Matt. 1:1; Gal. 3:16
Son of Isaac, Gen. 21:12	Luke 3:23; Matt. 1:2
Son of Jacob, Num. 24:17	Luke 3:23; Matt. 1:2
Tribe of Judah, Gen. 49:10	Matt. 1:2; Heb. 7:14
Family line of Jesse, Isa. 11:1	Luke 3:23; Matt. 1:6
House of David, Jer. 23:5; Ps. 132:11	Luke 3:23; Matt. 9:27
Born at Bethlehem, Mic. 5:2	Matt. 2:1; Luke 2:4
Presented with gifts, Ps. 72:10	Matt. 2:1, 11
Herod kills children, Jer. 31:15	Matt. 2:16
His pre-existence, Mic. 5:2; Isa. 9:6	Col. 1:17; John 1:1; Rev. 1:17
He will be called Lord, Ps. 110:1	Luke 2:11; Luke 20:41–44
He will be Immanuel, Isa. 7:14	Matt. 1:23; Luke 7:16
He will be a prophet, Deut. 18:18	Matt. 21:11; Luke 7:16; John 4:19
He will be a priest, Ps. 110:4	Heb. 3:1; Heb. 5:5–6
He will be a judge, Isa. 33:22	John 5:30; 2 Tim. 4:1
He will be a king, Ps. 2:6; Zech. 9:9	Matt. 27:37; 21:5; John 18:33–38
Anointed by Holy Spirit, Isa. 11:2	Matt. 3:16–17; Mark 1:10–11; John 1:32
His zeal for God, Ps. 69:9	John 2:15–17
Preceded by Messenger, Isa. 40:3	Matt. 3:1–2; 11:10; John 1:23
Ministry begins in Galilee, Isa. 9:1	Matt. 4:12, 13, 17
Ministry of miracles, Isa. 35:5–6	Matt. 9:32–33; Mark 7:33–35; John 5:5–9
Teacher of parables, Ps. 78:2	Matt. 13:34
Would enter the Temple, Mal. 3:1	Matt. 21:12
Would enter Jerusalem on donkey, Zech. 9:9	Luke 19:35–37; Matt. 21:6–11
"Stone of Stumbling" to Jews, Ps. 118:22	1 Pet. 2:7; Rom. 9:32–33
"Light" to Gentiles, Isa. 60:3; 49:6	Acts 13:47–48
Resurrection, Ps. 16:10; 30:3; 41:10	Acts 2:31; Luke 24:46; Mark 16:6
Ascension, Ps. 68:18	Acts 1:9
Seated at right hand of God, Ps. 110:1	Heb. 1:3; Mark 16:19; Acts 2:34–35
Betrayed by a friend, Ps. 41:9; 55:12–14	Matt. 10:4; 26:49–50; John 13:21
Sold for thirty pieces of silver, Zech. 11:12	Matt. 26:15; 27:3
Money to be thrown in God's house, Zech. 11:13	Matt. 27:5
Price given for potter's field, Zech. 11:13	Matt. 27:7
Forsaken by His disciples, Zech. 13:7; Mark 14:50; 14:27	Matt. 26:31
Accused by false witnesses, Ps. 35:11	Matt. 26:59–61
Dumb before accusers, Isa. 53:7	Matt. 27:12–19
Wounded and bruised, Isa. 53:5; Zech. 13:6	Matt. 27:26
Smitten and spit upon, Isa. 50:6; Mic. 5:1	Matt. 26:67; Luke 22:63

Mocked, Ps. 22:7–8	Matt. 27:31
Fell under the cross, Ps. 109:24–25	John 19:17; Luke 23:6; Matt. 27:31–32
Hands and feet pierced, Ps. 22:16; Zech. 12:10	Luke 23:33; John 20:25
Crucified with thieves, Isa. 53:12	Matt. 27:38; Mark 15:27–28
Prayed for His persecutors, Isa. 53:12	Luke 23:34
Rejected by His own people, Isa. 53:3	John 7:5, 48; Matt. 21:42–43
Friends stood afar off, Ps. 38:11	Luke 23:49; Mark 15:40; Matt. 27:55–56
People shook their heads, Ps. 109:25	Matt. 27:39
Stared upon, Ps. 22:17	Luke 23:35
Garments parted/lots cast, Ps. 22:18	John 19:23–24
To suffer thirst, Ps. 69:21; 22:15	John 19:28
Gall and vinegar offered to Him, Ps. 69:21	Matt. 27:34; John 19:28–29
His forsaken cry, Ps. 22:1	Matt. 27:46
Committed Himself to God, Ps. 31:5	Luke 23:46
Bones not broken, Ps. 34:20	John 19:33
Heart broken, Ps. 22:14	John 19:34
His side pierced, Zech. 12:10	John 19:34
Darkness over the land, Amos 8:9	Matt. 27:45
Buried in rich man's tomb, Isa. 53:9	Matt. 27:57–60

87   Peter W. Stoner, *Science Speaks* (Chicago: Moody, 1963), quoted in McDowell, *Evidence*, 175–176.

88   Stoner, *Science Speaks*.

QUESTION #3: DO ALL ROADS LEAD TO HEAVEN?

CHAPTER 15: ISN'T "ONLY ONE WAY" TOO NARROW?

89   "Medieval Sourcebook: Ambrose: Dispute with Symmachus," 414, http://www.fordham.edu/halsall/source/ambrose-sym.html.

90   Adapted from R. C. Sproul, *Reason to Believe* (Grand Rapids, MI: Zondervan, 1982), 41–43.

CHAPTER 16: WHAT DO MUSLIMS BELIEVE?

91   According to Phil Parshall (*New Paths in Muslim Evangelism: Evangelical Approaches to Contextualization* [Grand Rapids, MI: Baker, 1980], 142), "Muslims generally believe the dynamic of the Trinity consists of God the Father's having sexual intercourse with Mary the mother of Jesus, who was the second member of the Trinity. This union resulted in the birth of Jesus as the third person of the Godhead."

92   Efraim Karsh, *Islamic Imperialism* (London: Yale University Press, 2007), 14.

93   William L. Langer, ed., *An Encyclopedia of World History*, 6th ed. (New York: Houghton Mifflin, 2001), 108–109.

94   Karsh, *Islamic Imperialism*, 1.

CHAPTER 17: WHAT DO HINDUS BELIEVE?

95   See 1 Kings 17:17–24.

96   See 2 Kings 4:31–36.

97   See Acts 9:37–40.

98   See Acts 20:7–12.

99   The son of the widow of Nain (Luke 7:11–16), the daughter of Jairus (Mark 5:35–42), and Jesus's friend Lazarus (John 11:14–44).

CHAPTER 18: WHAT DO BUDDHISTS BELIEVE?

100   Quoted in Colin Chapman, *Christianity on Trial* (Herts, England: Lion, 1974), 226.

101   Steve Kumar, *Christianity for Skeptics* (Peabody, MA: Hurt Publishing, 2000), 129.

102   Anthony Flanagan, "Rebirth," http://buddhism.about.com/library/weekly/ aa071602a.htm.

CHAPTER 19: WHAT DO CHRISTIANS BELIEVE?

103   See 1 Corinthians 15:3–4.

104   See Acts 1:3, 9.

105   See Acts 2:1.

106   David Barrett and Todd Johnson's annual report, available at http://www.jesus.org.uk/dawn/2003/dawn16.html and http://gem-werc.org.

107   See Genesis 9:21–25.
108   See Revelation 7.
109   See Matthew 25:23.

CHAPTER 20: WHAT DO THE OTHER RELIGIONS BELIEVE?

110   www.adherents.com. Note: Adherents.com is a sociological site that analyzes religious groups and trends. The author of this book does not classify Latter-Day Saints (Mormons) and Jehovah's Witnesses as part of the Christian movement.
111   www.adherents.com/Religion_by_Adherents.html.

QUESTION #4: HOW CAN A GOOD GOD ALLOW SUFFERING?

CHAPTER 26: WHICH ACT ARE WE LIVING IN?

112   I am indebted to a sermon by Lee Strobel for this concept.

QUESTION #5: WHICH IS RIGHT: EVOLUTION OR CREATION?

CHAPTER 29: WHICH IS RIGHT: EVOLUTION OR CREATION?

113   I'm indebted to Phillip E. Johnson, *Darwin on Trial* (Downers Grove, IL: InterVarsity, 1993), 5, for these insights.
114   Francis S. Collins, *The Language of God* (New York: Free Press, 2007), 199.
115   Credit for this position is given to Phillip Johnson, whom I cited above.
116   Macroevolution refers to the development of a new type of species. Microevolution refers to adaptations within a species. Microevolution is evidenced by the wide variety of shapes, sizes, and specialties of dogs, cats, and other creatures as they have adapted to their environment.
117   R. Laird Harris, Gleason L. Archer Jr., and Bruce K. Waltke, *Theological Wordbook of the Old Testament*, v. 1 (Chicago: Moody, 1980), 370–371.

CHAPTER 30: DID OUR UNIVERSE HAVE A BEGINNING?

118   Steven Hawking and George Ellis, "The Cosmic Black-Body Radiation and the Existence of Singularities in Our Universe," *Astrophysical Journal*, 152 (April 1968): 25–36.
119   Bill Bryson, *A Short History of Nearly Everything* (New York: Random House, 2003), 10.
120   Bryson, *Short History*, 12.
121   See 1 Thessalonians 4:16.

CHAPTER 31: IF GOD MADE THE UNIVERSE, WHO MADE GOD?

122   Hugh Ross, *The Creator and the Cosmos* (Colorado Springs, CO: NavPress, 1995), 79.
123   I am indebted to Dr. Hugh Ross for this observation. For more of his thoughts on this, see *Creator and the Cosmos*, 79–81.
124   See Genesis 1:1.

CHAPTER 32: HOW DID IT ALL BEGIN?

125   See Genesis 22:17; 32:12.
126   Hugh Ross, *Genesis One: A Scientific Perspective* (Glendora, CA: Reasons to Believe, 2006), 10.
127   Ross, *Genesis One*, 11.
128   See Genesis 1:16–17.
129   I don't think Almighty God actually needed a rest. He rested as an example to us. In my book *I Love Sundays* (Colorado Springs, CO: Outreach, 2015), I document the physical, social, mental, and spiritual benefits of taking a Sabbath rest every seven days and how to do this in modern culture.

CHAPTER 33: HOW CAN YOU *NOT* BELIEVE IN EVOLUTION?

130   Richard Dawkins, *The Blind Watchmaker* (New York: Norton, 1986), 115.
131   Hubert Yockey, "A Calculation of the Probability of Spontaneous Biogenesis by Information Theory," *Journal of Theoretical Biology* 67 (1977): 377–378.
132   Robert Carter, PhD, ed., *Evolution's Achilles' Heels* (Creation Book Publishers, 2014), chapter 3.
133   Carter, chapter 1.
134   Carter, chapter 2.
135   Richard Dawkins, *River Out of Eden* (London: Weidenfeld & Nicholson, 1995), 133.
136   Susan Blackmore, "The World According to Dr. Susan Blackmore," *The Independent* (UK), January 21, 2004.
137   Carter, chapter 8.

138   Charles Darwin, *The Descent of Man*, 2nd ed. (London: John Murray, 1887), 156.

139   Simon Sebag Montefiore, *Young Stalin* (London: Weidenfeld & Nicholson, 2007), 40.

140   Carter, chapter 8.

141   This story was told by Mao's personal physician and is quoted from "The Great Dying," *The Sunday Mail*, Brisbane, Australia, February 2, 1997, 59–60, and cited in Carter, chapter 8.

142   C. S. Lewis, *God in the Dock* (Grand Rapids, MI: Eerdmans, 1970), 52–53.

CHAPTER 34: CAN SCIENCE AND SCRIPTURE GET ALONG?

143   If you don't remember much about Pascal's Triangle from your high school math classes, do a quick web search. It's a fun phenomenon!

144   Francis S. Collins, *The Language of God* (New York: Free Press, 2006), 15.

145   Collins, *Language of God*, 30.

146   Isaac Newton, *General Scholium*, trans. A. Motte (1825); *Newton's Principia: The Mathematical Principles of Natural Philosophy* (New York: Daniel Adee), 501. (The Greek word *pantokrator* is used by Paul in 2 Corinthians 6:18 and nine times by John in Revelation. The word is translated as "Almighty," and is only used of God.)

147   Johann Kepler, "Proem," *Harmonies of the World*, 1619.

148   Dr. Bence Jones, *The Life and Letters of Faraday*, vol. II (London: Green and Co., 1870), 325–326.

149   Lewis Campbell and William Garnet, *The Life of James Clerk Maxwell* (London: 1882; reprinted by Johnson Reprint Corporation, New York: 1969), 178.

150   Jeffrey Tomkins and Jerry Bergman, "Genomic Monkey Business—Estimates of Nearly Identical Human-Chimp DNA Similarity Re-Evaluated Using Omitted Data," *Journal of Creation*, 26(1):94–100, April 2012; creation.com/human-chimp-dna-similarity-re-evaluated.

151   Dr. Robert Carter presents a compelling case for the impossibility of humans evolving from chimps based on DNA dissimilarities in chapter 2 of *Evolution's Achilles' Heels*.

QUESTION #6: WHAT HAPPENS WHEN I DIE?

CHAPTER 37: WHAT WILL HELL BE LIKE?

152   See Acts 2:27, 31.

153   See Revelation 20:3.

CHAPTER 38: WHAT WILL THE NEW EARTH BE LIKE?

154   Randy Alcorn, in his book *Heaven* (Wheaton, IL: Tyndale, 2004), goes into greater detail on the geography of heaven on pages 250–251.

CHAPTER 39: WHAT WILL MY LIFE BE LIKE THEN?

155   See Philippians 3:21; Romans 6:4; 1 Corinthians 15:20.

156   See John 20:11–18.

157   See Luke 24:15–16.

158   See Luke 24:42–43.

159   See John 20:26.

160   C. S. Lewis, *The Weight of Glory* (New York: Macmillan, 1980), 18.

CHAPTER 40: HOW SHOULD I PREPARE FOR HEAVEN?

161   See Revelation 4:10.

162   See 2 Timothy 4:7–8.

163   See 1 Corinthians 9:24–25.

164   See Revelation 2:10.

165   See 1 Thessalonians 2:19–20.

166   See 1 Peter 5:1–4.

167   See Exodus 16:14–15.

168   Elisabeth Elliot, ed., *The Journals of Jim Elliot* (Grand Rapids, MI: Revell, 1978).